FINANCIAL SERVICES REGULATION
IN IRELAND –
THE ACCOUNTABILITY DIMENSION

Studies in Public Policy

The series *Studies in Public Policy* is published by the Policy Institute at Trinity College. It aims to bridge the gap between the academic and professional policy communities and make a real difference to public policy debate in Ireland. Each *Study* takes a practical policy problem and analyses it in a way that is academically rigorous yet accessible for all that.

Current and Forthcoming Titles

FINANCIAL SERVICES REGULATION IN IRELAND – THE ACCOUNTABILITY DIMENSION

Jonathan Westrup

Studies in Public Policy: 10

The Policy Institute

2002

First published 2002
by the Policy Institute
Trinity College, Dublin 2, Ireland
www.policyinstitute.tcd.ie

A catalogue record is available for this book from
the British Library

ISBN 1-902585-08-9

Cover design by Butler Claffey, Dublin
Origination by Carole Lynch, Dublin
Printed by ColourBooks Limited, Dublin

Contents

List of tables and figures

Abbreviations

C&AG   Comptroller and Auditor General
CBIFSA   Central Bank of Ireland and Financial Services Authority
CER   Commission for Energy Regulation
ESB   Electricity Supply Board
FSA   Financial Services Authority
GAO   General Accounting Office
IFSRA   Irish Financial Services Regulatory Authority
IOSCO   International Organisation of Securities Commissions
NAO   National Audit Office
ODTR   Office of the Director of Telecommunications Regulation
OECD   Office for Economic Co-operation and Development
Oftel   Office of Telecommunications
PAC   Public Accounts, Committee of
SEC   Securities and Exchange Commission
SME   Small and Medium Sized Enterprises
SMI   Strategic Management Initiative
SRA   Single Regulatory Authority
VFM   Value for Money

Executive summary

Research aims
The primary aim of this paper is to analyse the accountability structure of the Irish Financial Services Regulatory Authority (IFSRA), the new financial regulator. The accountability structure is divided into three parts:

1   the objectives of the regulator
2   the performance of the regulator
3   the methods by which it is to be scrutinised.

The paper also explains why a well-designed accountability structure will ensure that the IFSRA can be independent in the conduct of its duties and minimise the risk of regulatory capture.

Research findings
Before analysing the accountability structure, the paper outlines the rationale for financial regulation, the importance of financial services to the Irish economy and the evolution of the present regulatory structure. The research establishes that a financial regulator of the highest international standard is essential to maintaining the financial sector's continued success and good reputation. However, there is a general acceptance that the regulatory structure has been fragmented; with no one government department responsible for policy formulation, regulatory powers have been divided between different institutions and no single government department or regulator responsible for consumer protection.

The government recognised the need for a single regulatory authority in October 1998 when it established the Implementation Advisory Group. However, its subsequent decision in February 2001, and in legislative form in April 2002, to set up the IFSRA as part of a new regulatory and monetary authority, the Central Bank of Ireland and Financial Services Authority (CBIFSA), rather than as a stand-alone body as recommended by the Implementation Advisory Group, has important implications for the accountability structure of the new regulator. The Governor of the Central Bank is designated to be the chairman of the CBIFSA but under the provisions of the

Central Bank Act of 1998 will, in effect, be irremovable from office by the government. The paper asserts that these decisions mean that, despite the legislation's attempts to outline the duties and responsibilities of the IFSRA, there remain significant doubts about the new regulator's operational independence and considerable scope for confusion about lines of responsibility and accountability.

The paper makes three recommendations on the accountability structure of the IFSRA. First, the IFSRA must have clear and concise policy objectives. The CBIFSA Bill has proposed broad functions for the IFSRA that provide a basis for developing policy objectives. However, the proposed functions must be developed into more succinct objectives if they are to be of use in terms of accountability because objectives determine the role and rationale of an organisation and allow for evaluation of performance.

The research found that the existing Irish financial regulators lack clear and explicit objectives, as do the two utility regulators. This has created confusion about their role and their responsibilities. The paper recommends that an Oireachtas committee hold hearings during the CBIFSA Bill's legislative session allowing both practitioner and consumer groups to discuss the objectives of the new regulator.

Second, the IFSRA should publish a formal strategy statement. The CBIFSA Bill proposes that the IFSRA publish an annual strategic plan, which is to be welcomed. However, the plan must be part of a process that includes performance evaluation and the setting of performance targets. This process would ensure a consistency between the broad policy objectives and the work of the regulator, as well as making the task easier for those with the responsibility of scrutinising the performance of the IFSRA.

The final stage of the accountability structure is ensuring that the regulator is properly scrutinised. The primary means of scrutiny is the Oireachtas and in particular, the committee system. The paper suggests that the committee system is not properly resourced, as it is presently constituted, to undertake such a role. It finds that in comparison to a range of other parliaments, the committee system lacks access to expert advice and research. The paper recommends that the committee system investigates utilising the work of the Comptroller and Auditor General (C&AG) as a means to augment its research capability[1]. The experience of the New Zealand Audit

---

[1] The need for a consumer panel is particularly acute, given the lack of a developed consumer lobby in Ireland.

Office is cited as an example of how this recommendation could be pursued.

However, the paper acknowledges that there is evidence of a lack of interest by Oireachtas committees in undertaking a scrutiny role, indicated by gaps of as much as two years between meetings with regulators. It should be recognised, therefore, that extra resources may not guarantee a more efficient scrutiny role, if members of the Oireachtas do not wish to pursue such a role.

The paper also examines means by which citizens can participate in the scrutiny of the IFSRA. It welcomes the government's proposal to establish consumer and practitioner panels and recommends that they be given a statutory basis with their own research capability. It finds that the Irish utility regulators are unusual in an international context in not having established formal consumer panels.

Other means by which IFSRA could interact directly with the public are examined. These include the use of town meetings to allow for direct contact between the regulator and interested citizens and the use of surveys as a means of measuring both the performance of the regulator and the awareness of the public. The paper also suggests that the IFSRA should utilise the Internet to provide information for the public.

The proposal in the CBIFSA Bill that the IFSRA should have a statutory function to increase financial awareness is an important and welcome development in Irish financial regulation. The paper suggests that this should be one of the core statutory objectives of the IFSRA. The need to raise the level of financial awareness is of particular importance because of the increase in defined contribution pension schemes, where individuals are responsible for decisions about the investment strategy of their pensions.

The paper concludes by arguing that the political system's experience with regulators has not been wholly satisfactory and suggests that the cost of regulatory mistakes in financial services could be very high. The adoption of a well-defined accountability structure could help to avoid such problems in the very important area of financial regulation.

Acknowledgements

The research for this paper was carried out while I was a Visiting Research Fellow at the Policy Institute, Trinity College, Dublin. I would like to thank the Institute, and it former director, Professor Michael Laver, for the invitation. I would also like to thank, in particular, the Senior Research Officer, Úna Nic Giolla Choille, and her successor, Orla Lane, for their advice, encouragement and their editorial skills. I would also like to acknowledge the wise counsel and friendship of Dr Raj Chari of the political science department.

I am also greatly indebted to the many people who agreed to be interviewed for the purposes of the research. Their collective insights and observations were invaluable to me in preparing this paper. The views expressed are my own, as is responsibility for any errors.

Jonathan Westrup

1

Research purpose and outline

1.1 Purpose

The importance of regulation of the financial services sector has come to political prominence over the past decade as a range of financial controversies has come to light. The Taylor affair in 1996, where an insurance broker absconded with clients' funds, and allegations about overcharging by National Irish Bank in 1998, led to enquiries by Oireachtas committees amid concerns about the apparent lack of consumer protection in the regulatory structure. In particular, a report from the Oireachtas Joint Committee on Finance and the Public Service in July 1998 recommended that a single financial regulator be established (Oireachtas Committee on Finance and the Public Sector, 1998). The Committee argued that the existing regulatory structure was fragmented and that there was no agency with explicit responsibility for the protection of the consumer.

The government subsequently announced a decision to establish a Single Regulatory Authority (SRA) for financial services in October 1998 and asked an advisory group chaired by the Attorney General at that time, Michael McDowell, (the McDowell Report) to advise on its implementation.[2] The McDowell Report focused on the accountability of the SRA and recommended a structure by which it would be accountable to the executive, the Oireachtas and the judiciary. The Department of Finance proposed a different structure in February 2001. It proposed that the Irish Financial Services Regulatory Authority (IFSRA) be established as part of the Central Bank of Ireland and Financial Services Authority (CBIFSA) with the IFSRA responsible for financial regulation. These proposals were incorporated into the Central Bank and Financial Services Authority of Ireland Bill which was published in April 2002.

The primary aim of the paper is to identify and explore the conditions under which the new regulatory structure for the IFSRA

---

[2] The official title of the McDowell Report (1999) is the *Report of the Implementation Advisory Group on the Establishment of a Single Regulatory Authority for the Financial Services Sector*.

will deliver on accountability. In the view of the author, these conditions relate to the determination of objectives for the IFSRA, and the means by which it can be scrutinised both within the parliamentary process and directly by citizens.

1.2 Research methodology

The research methodology was made up of three components. The first was a literature review, the second a comparative analysis and the third was a series of interviews with key participants in the regulatory process.

The literature review was conducted under the following headings:

1   the academic discussion on regulation and accountability
2   the academic discussion on the role of regulators in the policy-making process
3   the role of the parliamentary committee system and its evolution in the comparator countries.

These headings covered the research areas relevant to the aims of the paper.

The countries selected for the comparative analysis were Australia, New Zealand and Britain. The comparator countries were chosen for two reasons. The first is that, like Ireland, they are states with a system of governance derived from the 'Westminster' model. While the institutional structure of each state has evolved differently, the underlying system of political accountability is broadly similar with a government that is accountable to parliament, which in turn is accountable to the electorate. Ministers are, in theory, responsible for deciding upon policy while the civil service is responsible for its enactment. This broad similarity in the structure of accountability allows for meaningful comparisons to be undertaken.

The second reason is that Britain and Australia have both fundamentally changed their financial regulatory structures in recent years. These changes offer interesting points of comparison for Ireland in determining an appropriate accountability structure.

The interview participants were chosen for their expertise and experience in the Irish regulatory system from both the practitioner and the policy perspectives. Interviewees with experience of the Irish committee system, either as politicians, staff or witnesses, were selected. In total, 24 interviews were undertaken.

The structured interviews had three purposes:

1   validating certain presumptions
2   gaining knowledge
3   obtaining comments on the feasibility of policy recommendations.

1.3 Structure

The structure of the remainder of the paper is outlined below.

Chapter 2 discusses the rationale for regulators in the political system, and analyses the concept of accountability and the requirement for balance between accountability and independence.

Chapter 3 analyses why financial regulation is necessary. It highlights the importance of the financial services sector to the Irish economy, and outlines the evolution of the present regulatory structure. The chapter compares the accountability structure suggested by the McDowell Report to that proposed by the Central Bank and Financial Services Authority of Ireland and the potential problems in the proposed accountability structure for the IFSRA.

Chapter 4 examines why a definition of specific policy objectives is central to the accountability structure of the IFSRA. It examines the objectives of financial regulators in the comparative countries and illustrates how they have influenced their style of regulation. The chapter concludes by analysing the effect of a lack of clear and concise objectives for the Central Bank and the utility regulators.

Chapter 5 examines why the development of a strategy statement is necessary to enhance the accountability structure. It discusses the significance of performance evaluation and the use of performance targets in the accountability process.

Chapter 6 examines the framework under which the IFSRA will be scrutinised by the Oireachtas committee system. It analyses the resources available to the committee system and compares them with those in the comparator countries.

Chapter 7 raises the importance of consumer and practitioner panels in providing for a complementary mechanism of accountability. It also examines how other direct methods of contact between the IFSRA and citizens could be utilised. The chapter concludes with a section discussing the need to raise the level of financial awareness.

Chapter 8 concludes the paper and reiterates that the IFSRA can only be accountable if it is given clear policy objectives and means by which its performance can be properly scrutinised.

2

Regulators and accountability

2.1 The role of regulators

The Irish political and administrative system is slowly coming to terms with the establishment of independent regulatory agencies. The focus on the role of regulators has been triggered by the creation of two utility regulators: the Office of the Director of Telecommunications Regulation (ODTR); and the Commission for Energy Regulation (CER).[3] The debate has tended to neglect the role of the Central Bank, which as a financial regulator has had responsibility for the prudential supervision of the banking system since 1971.

The government decision to remove the state monopoly in the telecommunication and electricity markets made the decision to establish independent regulators inevitable because of the conflict between the state's ownership of the utilities and its regulatory role. Article 157 of the Treaty of Rome instructs European regulators 'to neither seek nor take instruction from any government or from any other body' in the performance of their duties (Majone, 1996: 5-18).

The Irish political system is not alone in coming to terms with the role of regulators. The United States established its first independent regulatory commission, the Interstate Commerce Commission, as far back as 1887, but has a political system with a clear separation of powers (Keller, 1990). This means a different accountability structure from a Westminster system of government, because the regulatory commissions are accountable to Congress.

It was the privatisation programme of the public utilities in Britain, beginning with British Telecom in 1984, and the European Union's adoption of a policy of market liberalisation for the utility sector, that has brought the debate to Ireland. In the utility area, the European Union has determined that the state cannot be both the owner and the regulator of the utility.

---

[3] The government also established the Commission for Aviation Regulation in 2001. The Communications Regulation Bill (2002) incorporates the ODTR into the Communications Commission.

The remainder of this chapter outlines why independence and accountability are essential features of a regulatory system.

2.2 Independence

Majone (1996) summarises the reasons for the independence of regulators:

- a regulator has rule-making or adjudicative functions that would not be appropriate for either a government department or court
- a regulator needs access to a high level of expertise because of the complexity of regulatory issue
- a regulator can provide greater stability and continuity because it is removed from the electoral cycle.[4]

Fingleton (1999:10) defines independence in a regulatory context as meaning that

> regulation is carried out free of direction, influence or pressure and is guaranteed by statute in respect of the day-to-day responsibilities and functions of a regulator, within a legal framework that sets out policy objectives, duties and responsibilities.

The ODTR and the CER are both defined as independent in their enabling legislation. A financial regulator has the same requirement of independence as the utility regulators because it too has rule-making and adjudicative functions that require the level of independence defined by Majone.

2.3 Accountability

The perceived lack of accountability of the utility regulators has triggered debate and concern about who regulates the regulators. Former Attorney General David Byrne stated 'legislators should not stand over any system which takes away the rights of citizens to

---

[4] The political science academic literature increasingly uses a principal/agent framework to explain a government's decision to delegate powers to independent agencies such as regulators. For example, Thatcher and Stone Stewart (2002) argue that the government (as the principal) gains in delegating power to the regulator (as agent) because: it improves the credibility of policy; helps to overcome information asymmetries in technical areas of governance; enhances the efficiency of rule making; and helps the government to avoid taking the blame for unpopular decisions.

hold to account individuals who make decisions that affect their everyday lives' (Byrne, 1998). Michael McDowell, the Attorney General (1997-2002), declared 'the age of non-accountable power is over' (McDowell, 1999).

As Verheijen and Millar (1998: 97) point out, accountability has 'become one of the dominant themes in studies of public policy' as the structure of governance becomes increasingly complex and it becomes therefore more difficult to separate institutional responsibility for policy decisions. March and Olsen (1995: 152) state that the 'general principle is that anyone who has power within a democratic state should ultimately be accountable to the people for the exercise of that power'. They must 'report, explain and justify any exercise of authority; and submit to sanctions if necessary' (March and Olsen, 1995: 59).

Rhodes (1997) distinguishes between *political, managerial and legal* accountability.[5] Political accountability is defined as 'those with delegated authority being answerable for their actions to the people' while managerial accountability is defined as 'making those with delegated authority answerable for carrying out agreed tasks according to agreed criteria of performance' (Day and Klein, 1987: 27). Managerial accountability is often described as administrative accountability. Legal accountability is ensuring that those with delegated authority adhere to both Irish and international law. Peters divides accountability mechanisms between *ex ante* and *ex post*, with *ex ante* defined as the 'traditional rule-based' methods of specifying the duties and responsibilities of those with delegated authority, while *ex post* mechanisms are those designed to ensure that the duties and responsibilities have been carried out (Peters, 1996).

Rhodes (1997) argues that what he terms as the 'traditional mechanisms of accountability in representative democracy' are not designed to cope with 'multi-organizational, fragmented policy systems'. Western democracies have reacted in different ways to this challenge but Peters (1996) argues that a general theme has been an attempt to strengthen the role of *ex post* mechanisms such as audit offices, parliamentary committees and ombudsmen. These efforts can be understood as part of what Kettl describes as the 'global

---

[5] The focus of this paper is on the political and managerial accountability of the new financial regulator. It recognises that the McDowell Report and the Department of Finance have proposed mechanisms designed to ensure legal accountability.

public management revolution' (Kettl, 2000) and an attempt to improve and refine the methods of accountability described by Rhodes. An important example is an attempt to increase the level of citizen participation in policy-making and to create what Peters describes as 'the participatory state'.[6] Examples include the establishment of citizens' charters and the creation of consumer panels for regulatory agencies in Britain. Underpinning these efforts is Day and Klein's assertion that accountability has to be understood not only as the *right* to call people to account but also must be complemented 'by the notion of power as the *ability* to call people to account' (Day and Klein, 1987: 9).

2.4 Accountability in the Irish political system

The Irish political system has seen considerable change to both its *ex post* and *ex ante* mechanisms of accountability. The Strategic Management Initiative (SMI) was introduced in 1994 and foreshadowed the Public Services Management Act (1997). The rationale behind the SMI and the PSM was an attempt to define the *ex ante* responsibilities of those with delegated authority, because it asserted that ministers are responsible for choosing outputs and that public servants are responsible for producing the outputs (Boyle, 1998). The Act also determined that each department of state or scheduled office must publish a strategy statement every three years or within six months of the appointment of a new minister, '*that comprise the key objectives, outputs and related strategies (including use of resources)*' (Public Service Management Act 1997, Section 5.1 (a)). The Department of Public Enterprise proposed in March 2000 that strategy statements be extended to the utility regulators.[7]

The *ex post* mechanisms have also changed. The Ombudsman Act 1980 gave citizens a mechanism by which administrative actions can be investigated. The Comptroller and Auditor General (Amendment) Act 1993 widened the remit of the Comptroller and Auditor General (C&AG). The Oireachtas committee system has been strengthened by the Compellability of Witnesses Act 1997[8] and

---

[6] Peters (1996:47) describes it as 'the search for more political, democratic, and collective mechanisms for sending signals to government'.

[7] 'It is proposed that each regulator be required to adopt at regular intervals, strategy statements that reflect its statutory mandate and submit them to the minister'; Department of Public Enterprise (2000a:23).

[8] The full title of the Act is: Committees of the Houses of the Oireachtas (Compellability, Privileges and Immunities of Witnesses) Act, 1997.

the high visibility of the Public Accounts Committee report on the Deposit Interest Retention Tax controversy in 1999.[9] The Freedom of Information Act (1997) gives citizens powers to access certain government information.[10] The cumulative effect of these reforms is open to debate, but they provide the context in which the proposed accountability structure of the new financial regulatory structure can be analysed.

In the context of a regulator, similar issues of accountability arise whenever the state delegates specific powers to agencies. These are assessed in this paper in an analysis of both an *ex ante* and *ex post* framework of accountability. In general terms, they can be described as

> *ex ante:* the Oireachtas defines the authority that is delegated to the regulator in legislation. The legislation also determines the *ex post* mechanisms
>
> *ex post:* these are the control mechanisms by which the government and the Oireachtas attempts to ensure that the regulator fulfils its delegated functions. These include a requirement to report to the relevant government department, appear before certain Oireachtas committees and a requirement to account to the C&AG for the spending of public money. The decisions of a regulator are also subject to judicial review by the courts to ensure it does not exceed its legal authority.

This paper discusses the evolution of these mechanisms in relation to the utility regulators and attempts to assess their effectiveness as a means for ensuring both the accountability and independence of the new financial regulator. For a regulator to be accountable but also independent, the paper argues that the state must

1   define the role that the regulator is expected to perform, and clarify the differences between the role of government and the role of the regulator

2   ensure that there are mechanisms that function effectively, where the regulator can be asked to 'report,

---

[9] The Deposit Interest Retention Tax controversy arose over allegations in 1998 of widespread evasion of the tax by the use of non-resident deposits. See the Public Accounts Committee's Report *Parliamentary Inquiry into DIRT: First Report 1999* for a full description.

[10] Verheijen and Millar (1998) and Dooney and O'Toole (1999) describe, in detail, the changes to these accountability mechanisms.

explain and justify' the exercise of its authority (Majone, 1996: 59).

2.5 Regulatory risks

It is clear from the experience of the utility regulators in Britain that defining the respective roles of the government and a regulator is not an easy task.[11] However, with the appropriate *ex ante* and *ex post* accountability mechanisms, three potential risks to good governance from regulation can be minimised:

1   the danger to which Byrne and McDowell refer of unaccountable authority (see Section 2.3)
2   the risk of inappropriate government intervention in the regulatory process
3   the risk of 'regulatory capture'

A regulator that is not accountable to the political process is at variance with the basic tenet of democratic theory as described earlier: 'the general principle is that anyone who has power within a democratic state should ultimately be accountable to the people for the exercise of that power' (March and Olsen, 1995: 152). As both the comments of Byrne and McDowell indicate and the government's explicit remit to the Implementation Advisory Group on the establishment of a Single Regulatory Authority confirms, the objective of accountability for the financial regulator has had a high political priority.[12]

A clearly defined structure of accountability will also minimise the risk of inappropriate political intervention in financial regulation. There may be little or no evidence of such political intervention in the past but, given the significance and sensitivity of financial regulation, it is important to design a structure to ensure that it cannot occur. A clearly defined structure also reduces the need for what the OECD terms 'the command and control reflex', which it describes as 'looking first to regulatory solutions rather than other types of policy instruments (or no intervention), [that] is still present among [Irish] parliamentarians and regulators' (OECD, 2001: 49). An accountability structure that has clearly defined

---

[11] For an excellent exposition of the controversies in Britain, see Vogel (1996).

[12] *Report of the Implementation Advisory Group on the Establishment of a Single Regulatory Authority for the Financial Services Sector* (1999); its remit included 'the organisational structure for the authority including the manner of its public accountability' (p. 91).

responsibilities should reduce the desire or the apparent need to intervene.

Regulatory capture, where a regulator is 'captured' by producer interests is a recognised phenomenon in the regulatory literature.[13] Fingleton, Evans and Hogan (1998: 26) define regulatory capture as a 'situation in which a market regulator largely reflects the interests of the regulated industry in its actions instead of the interests of consumers'. The OECD (2001) considers that the Irish regulatory bodies 'need to be vigilant to avoid capture by producer interests' which 'tend to take precedence over consumer interests'.

2.6 Conclusion
This chapter argues that the accountability structure of the financial regulator must be designed to ensure a delicate balance between independence and accountability. A financial regulator must be independent because of its specific rule-making and adjudicative functions. However, with the appropriate *ex ante* and *ex post* mechanisms, independence does not imply that a regulator cannot be accountable to the political process.

While the design of such mechanisms is not straightforward, the chapter asserts that they will minimise the risk of a regulator assuming unaccountable authority, of political interference in the regulatory process and of the emergence of regulatory capture.

---

[13] See Stigler (1971).

3

Financial regulation: rationale and evolution in Ireland

3.1 Chapter outline

Before beginning an analysis of the accountability structure in the next chapter, this chapter outlines the rationale for financial regulation and how the regulatory structure has evolved in Ireland. It begins with a description of the rationale for financial regulation and then defines what is meant by the term financial services and the importance of those services to the Irish economy. The chapter then analyses the recent evolution of the structure of regulation, contrasting the accountability structure proposed by the McDowell Report with the structure proposed by the Central Bank and Financial Services Authority of Ireland Bill in the creation of the IFSRA.

3.2 The rationale for financial regulation

The rationale for financial regulation is based on two concerns:

- the particular role that the banking system plays in the economy and the concept of systemic risk (where the failure of an individual financial institution leads in a sequential fashion to similar adverse consequences for other financial institutions, introducing the possibility of system-wide failures)
- the concept of asymmetric information, which assumes that the purchasers of financial products find it difficult both to assess the risks and returns of transactions they undertake and to assess the safety and soundness of financial firms.

The first rationale recognises the pivotal role of banks in an economy in so far as they are 'potentially subject to runs which may have contagious effects.' (Llewellyn, 1999:13). This concern was a vital factor in the Central Bank and the then government's decision to intervene in 1985 following the insolvency of the Insurance Corporation of Ireland. The concept of asymmetric information assumes that consumers are less well-informed than are suppliers of financial services, due in part to the complexity of the products but also due to the long-term nature of many financial contracts. Llewellyn argues that there are also potential principal-agent problems in the sale of financial services because of potential conflicts of interest in the relationship between the seller and the purchaser of financial products. (Llewellyn, 1999) The role of a regulator is therefore 'to correct for market imperfections or market failures which would compromise consumer welfare in a regulation-free environment' (Llewellyn, 1999: 9).

However, in designing a financial regulatory structure, there are two important principles that must be considered. The first principle relates to the concept of proportionality, where the benefits produced by regulation must justify the costs. In terms of financial regulation, proportionality means that a system cannot be designed to ensure that there is no risk of failure because the cost of such a system would greatly outweigh the benefits. The second principle is that of *caveat emptor* or buyer beware. A regulatory system, while protecting the interests of the buyers of financial products, must operate on the basis that the buyer must make every practical effort to understand the risks that are undertaken.[14]

3.3 A definition of financial services and their role in the Irish economy

There is no simple definition of what constitutes the financial services sector in Ireland. It is made up of a wide range of financial activities that include banking, insurance and stockbroking, and entities as diverse as building societies, credit unions and moneylenders. The traditional divisions in the provision of financial services are disappearing as financial institutions merge and attempt to provide a comprehensive range of services.

The importance of a high standard of financial regulation in the development of financial services has been widely recognised in Ireland: 'an effective yet responsive system of regulation is viewed as one of Ireland's strongest sources of competitive advantage in the

---

[14] The paper argues in Chapter 6 that the new regulator should be given a statutory objective of raising the level of financial awareness.

international financial services sector' (Department of the Taoiseach, 2000). However, by the nature of the activities of financial services companies, the focus of Irish financial regulation has been on prudential, rather than consumer regulation. This has meant an emphasis on the need to avoid systemic risk and countering the problem of asymmetric information by regulation rather than education.

The Irish government has pursued a strategy of promoting the development of financial services since 1987 that has been 'demonstrably successful' (Kearney, 1999: 174), as proven by the growth in employment in the sector, from 114,300 in 1994 to over 228,000 by the end of 2001.[15] The focus of the strategy has been on developing the Irish Financial Services Centre by attracting financial services companies with low rates of corporation tax.[16] The success of the strategy can be measured by the fact that the IFSC employs 11,000 people and raised corporation tax revenues of over six hundred million euro in 2001.[17]

Table 1: Corporation tax

Year	1997	1998	1999	2000
Euros(million)	2,154	2,614	3,442	3,855
Percentage of Total from IFSC	15	14	16	12

Source: Revenue Commissioners (2001), *Statistical Bulletin 2000*, Dublin: Revenue Commissioners. IFSC data are Revenue Commissioners estimates.

The ESRI has predicted that if the present rate of employment growth continues, financial services will employ more people than agriculture by 2005 (Kearney, 1999, p. 176).

---

[15] Estimates from the Central Statistics Office, Dublin.
[16] The IFSC was established in 1987 with the aim of developing international financial services capability in Ireland.
[17] Estimates from the *Financial Services Industry Association Annual Report 2001* and the Revenue Commissioners.

3.4 The evolution of the existing regulatory framework

The structure of regulation of the financial sector, prior to the government's February 2001 decision and subsequent legislation to reorganise the sector, is best described as fragmented. The responsibility for the legal framework, and therefore policy formulation, for financial regulation has been divided primarily between the Department of Finance and the Department of Enterprise, Trade and Employment. Table 2 itemises their specific responsibilities.

Table 2: Framework of financial regulation

Department of Finance	• Responsible for the legal framework for the Central Bank (regulator) • Supervises directly banks and building societies. [(1)] • Authorises and supervises investment intermediaries, stockbrokers and exchanges.
Department of Enterprise, Trade and Employment	• Legal framework • Legislative framework for Director of Consumer Affairs • Regulator for insurance undertakings

Source: Report of the Implementation Advisory Group on the Establishment of a Single Regulatory Authority for the Financial Services Sector (1999), Dublin: Stationery Office.
Note: [(1)] The Department of Environment and Local Government is responsible for the overall legislative framework for building societies.

The Department of Enterprise, Trade and Employment has been responsible for both policy formulation and regulation in the insurance area.[18] The IMF states 'this location of the supervisor (regulator) within a Ministry means that it is not a fully independent entity' (International Monetary Fund, 2001; quotation from Table 1, 'Ireland: Observance of IAIS Insurance Supervisory Principles–Summary Assessment'). An important part of the

---

[18] This combination of responsibilities is extremely unusual in an international context.

financial regulatory system has therefore not been independent as Majone (1996) and Fingleton (1999) define the term.

The Central Bank has had statutory responsibility for the direct supervision of virtually all financial institutions in Ireland with the exception of insurance undertakings with 'a trend in recent years to concentrate the prudential regulation of financial institutions in the Bank' (McDowell Report, 1999: 5). The Central Bank, according to the C&AG, considers that its regulatory objectives are to ensure as far as possible that

- individual financial institutions comply with a set of rules that are designed to ensure their continuing solvency and liquidity (prudential supervision)
- risks to the financial system as a whole are minimised (systemic supervision)
- there is a degree of protection for depositors with credit institutions and for clients of investment firms (conduct of business supervision) (Comptroller and Auditor General, 1999b, Section 1.7).

There has been no one institution with responsibility for consumer regulation, which has been divided between the Central Bank, the Director of Consumer Affairs and the Department of Enterprise, Trade and Employment. In this capacity, the Central Bank has had a very limited role in consumer regulation. It is responsible for conduct of business rules, various compensation schemes and maintains registers 'to enable the consumer to determine which firms are authorised' (McDowell Report: 11). The Director of Consumer Affairs has a range of powers under various Acts of the Oireachtas, in particular the Consumer Credit Act of 1995. This gives the Director the power to regulate the level of bank charges. The Department of Enterprise, Trade and Employment administers the Consumer Credit Act and the Consumer Information Act of 1978 that prohibits misleading advertising.

3.5 Assessment of prudential regulatory structure

The focus on the need for a change in the regulatory structure has concentrated on the role of the consumer. There has been little public discussion about the prudential side of regulation because the rate of failure among financial institutions has been low.

However, as the C&AG's report on the Central Bank argued, the fact that there has been a very low level of prudential failure does not mean that it can be assumed that prudential regulation is beyond criticism. The report recommended that 'a more comprehensive set of measures should be developed' to identify 'the contribution of the Bank's risk management activities to the level of stability achieved' (Comptroller and Auditor General, 1999b: 40).

The Central Bank responded to the C&AG's review and set up a Financial Services Policy Committee in January 2000 'to better coordinate supervisory activities' and 'additional steps were taken to enhance the "risk-based approach" to supervision' (International Monetary Fund 2001, Paragraph 32). The IMF in its inspection found the Central Bank to be fully compliant with the Basle Core Principles for effective banking supervision (IMF 2001).[19]

However, the IMF report considered that in the area of insurance regulation, Ireland 'may need to consider more stringent requirements to address the risks that could be inherent in a rapidly growing and increasingly complex insurance sector' (IMF, 2001, Executive Summary, Review of IAIS Insurance Supervisory Principles). The report specifically mentions 'the location of a supervisor within a Ministry means that it is not a fully independent entity'. It also comments on 'the limited resources to carry out a formal inspection programme' and that 'there is no formal programme in place and limited capacity in practice to direct and monitor the internal control systems of insurers'.

Given the importance of financial regulation, the government's decision to set up a single regulator should include a commitment to subject the IFSRA to a regular external audit of its regulatory capability.

3.6 The recent evolution of financial regulation

Given the 'multiplicity of bodies' that has made up the structure of the financial regulatory framework, it is no surprise that a 'consumer gap' emerged (John Corcoran, quoted in *Report of the Oireachtas Joint Committee on Finance and the Public Service*, 1999). The recognition of such a gap in financial regulation for the consumer was recognised as far back as the Oireachtas debate on the Central Bank Act of 1989 as the following quotes indicate.

---

[19] The Bank for International Settlements (BIS), through its Basel Committee, has outlined twenty-five core principles for effective banking supervision. See http://www.big.org.

- There has never been an adequate debate in this House on the accountability of the Central Bank for the discharging of its functions (Michael McDowell, in Oireachtas Report, 1989:1918).
- There is a gaping hole in financial protection for the consumer, the investor (McDowell, ibid: 1913).
- A piecemeal approach to the supervisory functions of the Central Bank will lead to a major investment scandal here (McDowell, ibid: 1913).

The last decade has seen a series of legislative measures designed to improve the level of financial protection for consumers, with the primary catalyst for change being a series of European Union Directives. The one major domestic piece of legislation was the Consumer Credit Act of 1995.

The first catalyst for change was the Taylor affair in 1996, where a former chairman of the Irish Brokers Association (IBA) absconded with clients' funds. The Select Committee on Enterprise and Economic Strategy held hearings on the implications of the issue and issued a report in May 1997 which recommended that the Central Bank should take responsibility for all financial regulation. The government announced in January 1997 that responsibility for regulation of investment intermediaries was to be transferred from a self-regulatory structure under the IBA to the Central Bank.

The Governor of the Central Bank stated at the time that 'we all recognise that there is a gap in the system', meaning the protection of the consumer. He also stated 'the essence of consumer regulation centres around access to information, standards of transparency and the right of appeal' (Maurice O'Connell, in evidence to Joint Committee on Enterprise and Economic Strategy, October 1996, Oireachtas Report.) It is also evident that a relative neglect of the interests of consumers has been reflected in other areas of Irish regulatory policy. The OECD has asserted, 'consumer interests are not well represented in policy debate and deliberation in Ireland, which remains dominated by producer interests' (OECD, 2001: 105).

The second major catalyst for change was the allegations against National Irish Bank (NIB) in March of 1998. These allegations prompted the Committee of Finance and the Public Sector to hold hearings and to issue a report which was published in July 1998. The Committee, having heard evidence and studied various European financial regulatory systems, recommended in its report,

The Regulation and Supervision of Financial Institutions, that a single financial regulator be established (Oireachtas Committee on Finance and the Public Sector, 1998).

The initial NIB allegations also prompted the Minister for Finance to appoint a working group on 'Banking and Consumer Issues' in April 1998, whose brief according to the General Secretary of the Department of Finance was 'a systematic overview of the fit between the Central Bank and the Director of Consumer Affairs' (Paddy Mullarkey, in evidence to Joint Committee on Finance and the Public Service, 1998, in *Report of the Implementation Advisory Group*). The working group's report did not contain recommendations because it was overtaken by the decision in October 1998 to set up a Single Regulatory Authority (Working Group on Banking and Consumer Issues, Department of Finance (under FOI), 1998).

The Oireachtas Committee's recommendation that a single regulator be appointed was a crucial factor in the government's decision to specify in its brief to the Implementation Advisory Group that a single regulatory agency be appointed.[20] The Committee's recommendation followed an investigation into changes in financial regulation in other European Union member states. Sweden and Denmark were the first EU states to introduce a single regulator, followed by the UK. The rationale for a single regulator has been, according to Briault, 'a concern that a fragmented regulatory structure might generate inconsistencies in approach, insufficient communication or an inadequate overview of regulated firms as more financial conglomerates emerge' (Briault, 1999: 14).

The government, in October 1998, appointed a Single Regulatory Authority Implementation Advisory Group, chaired by the Attorney General Michael McDowell, with a wide-ranging remit on how the SRA should be established. The remit included a specific request to comment on 'the organisational structure for the authority, *including the manner of its public accountability'*. The Group published its recommendations in May 1999 in what became known as the McDowell Report.

---

[20] This point was confirmed to the author by a number of interviewees.

3.7 McDowell Report: recommendations on accountability

The McDowell Report recommended the setting-up of a new single regulatory authority (SRA) with responsibility for 'all financial service providers'. The report argued that 'the SRA should have a high degree of accountability to the people through the Minister for Finance and the Oireachtas' (McDowell Report, 1999: 45) and made detailed recommendations on a proposed accountability structure.

3.7.1 Ex ante mechanisms

The report stated that 'the SRA should have clear statutory responsibility for the implementation of regulation and supervision of financial services within its remit' (McDowell Report, 1999: 45). The Minister for Finance should be the sole minister with responsibility for the SRA and should appoint six members of a nine-member public interest board.

3.7.2 Ex post mechanisms

The report recommended a range of *ex post* mechanisms:

- publication of an annual report
- members of the SRA should appear before 'a relevant Joint Committee of the Oireachtas whenever requested' (McDowell Report, 1999: 50)
- establishment of consumer and industry panels
- appointment of a Financial Services Ombudsman
- establishment of an independent appeals tribunal
- audit by the C&AG (including the option of a Value for Money mandate)
- annual budgetary approval from the Minister for Finance
- the right of the Minister for Finance to be consulted 'in regard to the execution and performance of any function or duty' (McDowell Report, 1999: 50) of the SRA.

Figure 1: The McDowell Report's alternative model

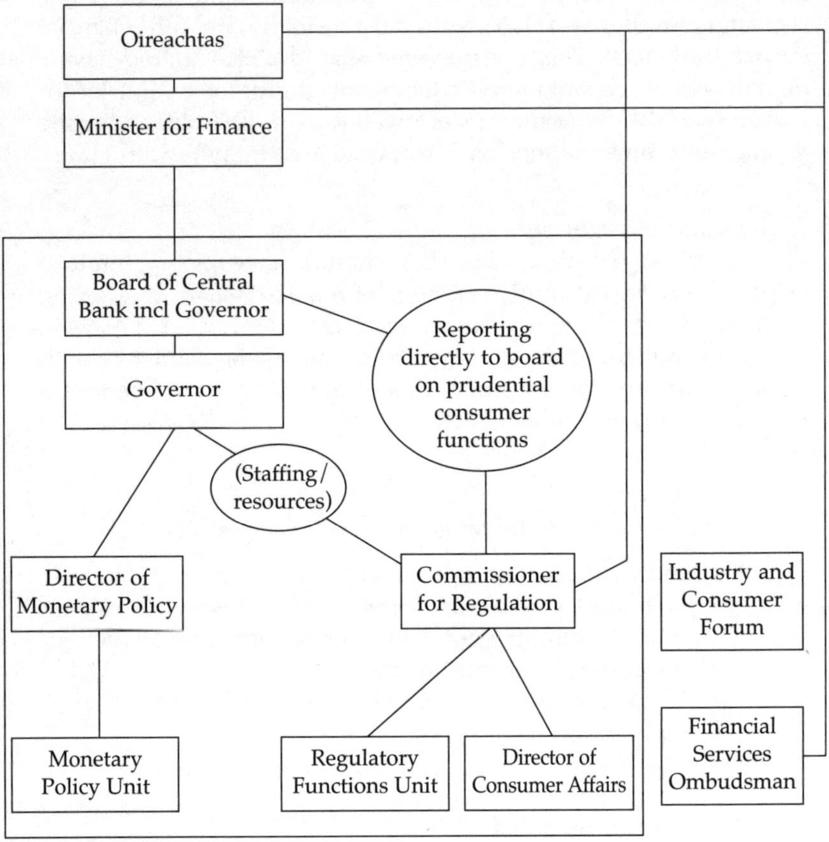

Source: Report of the Implementation Advisory Group on the Establishment of a Single Regulatory Authority for the Financial Services Sector (1999), the McDowell Report, p. 81.

The Report also contained a minority 'alternative model' (see Figure 1) that recommended the establishment of the SRA within the Central Bank. A Commissioner for Regulation would be appointed by the Central Bank board and 'would have autonomy insofar as *the* operation of the regulatory system would be concerned' (McDowell Report, 1999: 79). The minority model adopted the other *ex post* accountability mechanisms suggested in the report.

3.8 The Central Bank and Financial Services Authority of Ireland Bill

The government, in proposals first published in February 2001, and amended in the Central Bank and Financial Services Authority of Ireland Bill[21] in April 2002, has recommended a different regulatory structure (see Figure 2) to that of the majority view of the McDowell report but has maintained many of the *ex post* accountability mechanisms. In place of a 'stand alone' Single Regulatory Authority, the Department proposes the establishment of an Irish Financial Services Regulatory Authority (IFSRA) that is accountable to both the Minister for Finance and the Oireachtas for prudential regulation and customer protection, but also to a new entity termed the Central Bank of Ireland and Financial Services Authority (CBIFSA).

CBIFSA's *ex ante* accountability will be derived from the statutory authority that is to be delegated to it in the CBIFSA Bill. IFSRA's *ex ante* accountability will be derived from its statutory mandate.

The CBIFSA Bill proposes a series of the McDowell *ex post* mechanisms for the IFSRA including the independent appeals tribunal, the publication of a separate annual report for IFSRA, an obligation to appear before an Oireachtas committee and ministerial approval of IFSRA's budget. However, the setting up of the Financial Services Ombudsman and the industry and consumer panels will be dealt with in a later Bill.

---

[21] This is termed the CBIFSA Bill in the remainder of the paper.

Figure 2: Department of Finance proposed financial regulatory structure

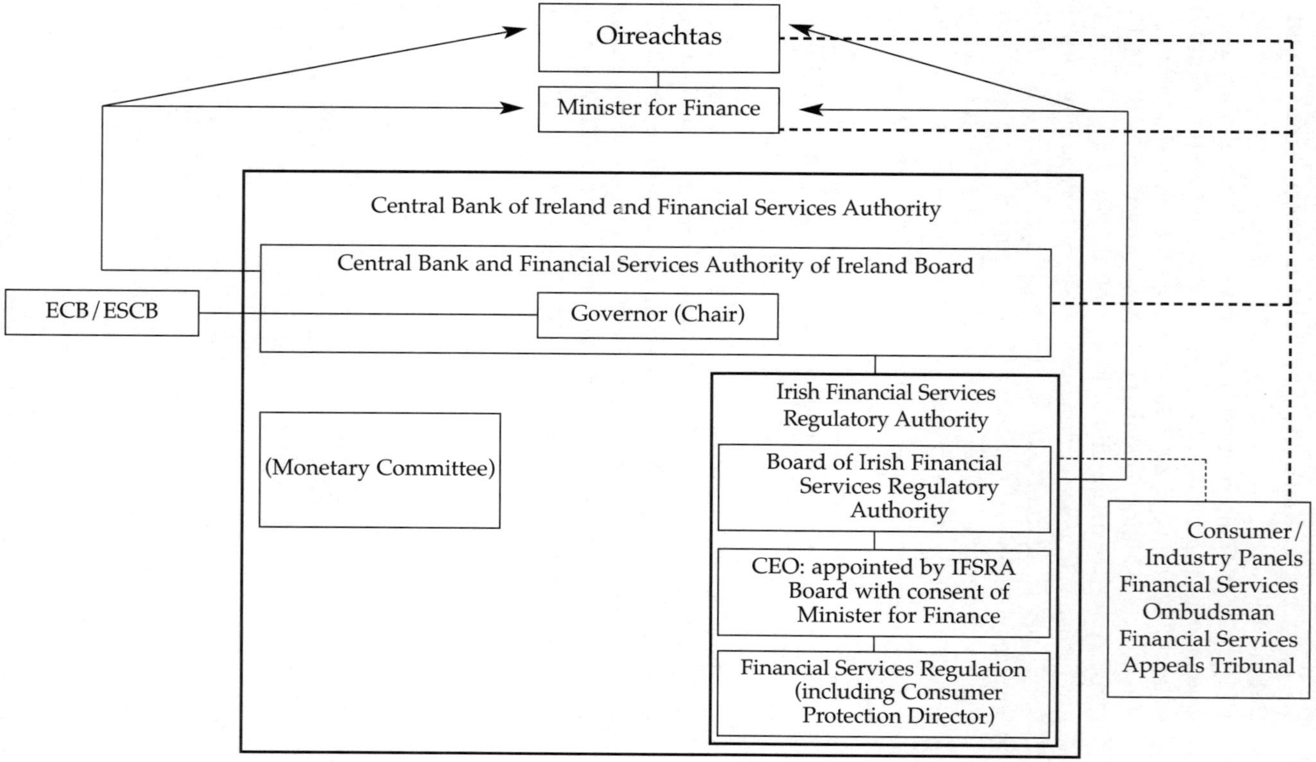

Source: Department of Finance

3.9 Differences between McDowell Report and the CBIFSA Bill

The McDowell Report proposed that the SRA should be independent of the Central Bank, laying great emphasis on concerns about the accountability of a regulatory structure within the Central Bank. This concern stemmed, according to the report, from 'in particular, the constraints imposed by the Maastricht Treaty' (McDowell Report, 1999: 46). The report quotes Dr John Breslin that, under the provisions of the 1998 Central Bank Act, 'sole power regarding ECSB and ECB matters vest solely in the Governor of the Central Bank' (McDowell Report, 1999: 47). This led the report to conclude that 'the Central Bank, as presently constituted with the Governor as Chairman and Chief Executive, who is effectively irremovable from office and who is accountable to the Oireachtas only in a limited way, does not afford the degree of accountability recommended by the Group' (McDowell Report, 1999: 48).

The government's decision to set up a new entity, CBIFSA, is an attempt to overcome this difficulty, with IFSRA having its own reporting structures to the Minister for Finance and the Oireachtas. However, it is proposed that the CBIFSA retain responsibility for

- promoting financial stability through co-ordination of monetary and regulatory function[22]
- promoting the development within the state of the financial services industry (but in such a way as not to affect the objective of the Bank in contributing to the stability of the state's financial system) (Central Bank and Financial Services Authority of Ireland Bill, 2002).

It is usual that the Central Bank retains overall responsibility for financial stability when a single regulatory authority is created (Briault, 1999). However, given the overall responsibilities of CBIFSA, the government and the Oireachtas will be delegating significant regulatory authority to an institution which is chaired by a governor who is 'effectively irremovable from office' (McDowell Report, 1999: 48). The consequences of such a structure appear to be that in the event of a significant failure in the regulatory system, the government and the Oireachtas could remove the board of the

---

[22] The Central Bank and Financial Services Authority Bill states that CBIFSA will 'carry out the efficient and effective coordination of the activities of the constituent parts of the Bank (Section 6 of Bill, substitution of Section 5A of the Central Bank Act, 1942).

IFSRA, but could not remove the chair of CBIFSA. Such a situation could be potentially very damaging to the IFSRA's credibility as a financial regulator.

The McDowell report (1999) argued that the benefits of establishing a new and independent organisation would

- provide for singularity of purpose in relation to regulation and customer protection in financial services
- provide a coherent, robust and transparent approach to financial regulation which would promote public and institutional confidence in the financial services industry and in the regulatory process
- provide for the development of a separate corporate identity that would help attract and motivate high quality staff and help to develop staff loyalty
- ensure that all staff would enter the new body on a basis of equality of opportunity which would enhance their commitment to the new body.

The government's decision not to adopt the McDowell Report's majority recommendation of a stand-alone regulator, but to decide upon a structure that is close, if not quite identical to the minority report, means that these benefits may well be foregone.

The legislation does set out in considerable detail the role and responsibilities of the IFSRA. However, given the institutional design of CBIFSA, it remains very difficult to argue that IFSRA maintains any meaningful operational independence. From an accountability perspective, the 'effectively irremovable' governor who chairs CBIFSA remains an important potential stumbling block. It is, above all, a structure that appears to offer considerable potential for confusion about responsibility and accountability.

3.10 Conclusion
This chapter argues that there are two concerns that underlie the need for financial regulation; the concepts of systemic risk and asymmetric information. It then defines financial services, outlines their significance to the Irish economy and suggests that a high standard of regulation is very important to the further development of financial services. The paper suggests that the proposed new regulator should be subject to a regular external audit of its prudential performance to ensure that high standards are achieved.

The analysis of the existing structure of financial regulation indicates that it has been fragmented, with three different government departments involved in policy formulation. It is also clear that no one institution has had responsibility for consumer protection and that regulation of the insurance industry has not been independent of government. The chapter has also concluded that it was the emergence of two apparent financial crises that was the catalyst for proposed change in the regulatory structure rather than a realisation of the inadequacy of the existing system.

The government's decision not to accept the McDowell Report recommendation that the new regulator should be a 'stand-alone' body has important implications for the IFSRA's accountability structure. In particular, the decision that the Governor of the Central Bank should be the chair of the CBIFSA implies that a key member of the new regulatory structure will not be removable from office by the government or the Oireachtas. The consequence of these decisions is that although the legislation designates the duties and functions of the IFSRA, there remains considerable risk to the new regulator's operational independence because of the lack of clear lines of responsibility and accountability.

4

The importance of policy objectives

4.1 Introduction

This chapter examines why the government must specify policy objectives for the IFSRA. It argues that policy objectives are the key initial step in ensuring that a regulator is accountable. They are the essential *ex ante mechanism* of an accountability structure because they define and circumscribe 'the exercise of authority' (March and Olson, 1995) and therefore the nature and scope of the role that the state is delegating to the regulator.

The importance of objectives is illustrated by reference to the experience of the comparator countries and how they have determined the style of financial regulation. The chapter argues that neither the Department of Finance nor the Central Bank has made sufficiently explicit their policy objectives concerning financial regulation. The chapter also refers to the Irish utility regulators and argues that the government has not set them explicit policy objectives.

The chapter stresses the need for a debate about the policy objectives as part of the legislative process and argues that such a debate will ensure that the new financial regulator has a level of political legitimacy.

4.2 The importance of objectives

There is widespread acceptance of the importance of policy objectives for all public organisations. The government has acknowledged their importance for all government departments and agencies in the Strategic Management Initiative (SMI) and the Public Service Management Act of 1997. The Act determines that each department of state or scheduled office must publish a strategy statement every three years or within six months of the appointment of a new minister *'that comprise the key objectives, outputs and related strategies (including use of resources)'* (Public Service Management Act, 1997, Section 5.1 (a)). The Department of

Public Enterprise has proposed that strategy statements be extended to the utility regulators.[23]

The Department's proposal follows that of the OECD which, in its report on regulatory reform, recommended that governments 'adopt at the political level, broad programmes of regulatory reform *that establish clear objectives* and frameworks for implementation'. It clarifies that 'good regulation should be needed *to serve clearly identified policy goals*' (OECD, 1997c: 37, emphasis added). Objectives must also be as specific as possible and must be consistent with each other if they are to be useful to an organisation.

4.3 The objectives of the existing system of financial regulation

The policy objectives of the present structure of financial regulation are gradually being stated in a more explicit fashion. The Department of Finance, which has legislative responsibility for the Central Bank, in its Statement of Strategy for 2001-2003, outlines 'policy in relation to Financial Services' as part of its first Strategic Priority (Department of Finance Strategy Statement, 2001-2003). The Statement outlines:

> in developing policies to underpin the effective prudential and systemic regulation of the financial services sector, with particular regard to the needs of the consumer, to support and encourage financial stability; a competitive, efficient market in financial services; and best practice across the industry from a customer perspective.

The indicator of progress is public confidence in the financial services sector. Financial regulation at EU level is also part of the third Strategic Priority. Under the title 'EU-wide financial services regulation', the Department of Finance's objective is

> to consult appropriately within Ireland and to participate at EU level in the consultative and decision-making processes in relation to EU-wide financial services regulation; and to support the development of, and to implement in a timely fashion, the EU Financial Services Action Plan.

---

[23] 'It is proposed that each regulator be required to adopt at regular intervals, strategy statements that reflect its statutory mandate and submit them to the minister.' (Department of Public Enterprise, 2000a: 23).

This latest Strategy Statement is in marked contrast to that for 1998-2000 where financial regulation was mentioned just twice. The longest reference was under the general heading of European Union participation and had the objective

> to contribute effectively to the development of European Union policy on the regulation of the financial system and to formulation of proposals for an effective and competitive system of financial regulation (Department of Finance Strategy Statement, 1998-2000).

The second reference stated that the Department provides 'the necessary legislative framework for financial regulation' (Department of Finance Strategy Statement, 1998-2000). There was no mention of either a consumer or customer perspective.

The Central Bank, the most important regulatory agency, in its strategy statement published in 1999, states that it is committed to 'protecting the stability of the banking and securities systems' (Central Bank of Ireland Strategy Statement, 1999).[24] A Value for Money (VFM) report from the C&AG stated that 'the fundamental objectives of financial regulation are *derived* from legislation and are *captured* in the overall mission statement of the Bank and in strategic statements for the two departments in the Supervision Division' (Comptroller and Auditor General, December 1999b: 2.1, emphasis added). The International Monetary Fund stated that 'the broad objectives of banking supervision ... are *defined* and *disclosed* in the Irish statutes, including Acts and Regulations, implementation of EU directives and corresponding amendments' (International Monetary Fund, 2001, Paragraph 3, emphasis added).

The Department of Enterprise, Trade and Employment has, as two of its five strategic objectives:

- to foster the well-being of consumers by promoting competition in all sectors of the economy and by such other measures as are necessary to ensure that consumers derive the maximum benefit from the operation of the market
- to effect a business regulatory system which is to the forefront of international standards, commands public

---

[24] The Central Bank has been awaiting the publication and enactment of the CBIFSA Bill before it publishes a further strategy statement.

confidence and international respect (the Department of Enterprise, Trade and Employment web-site, 2002).[25]

It is difficult to describe the strategy statements of the Department of Finance and the Central Bank as meeting the Public Sector Management Act's criteria of comprising 'key objectives, outputs and related strategies to be achieved' in terms of financial regulation. However, the Department of Finance's latest strategy statement does lay out objectives in a more explicit fashion than its previous statement. The Central Bank can legitimately point out that ensuring a high standard of financial regulation has always been an important policy objective but its present strategy statement does not reflect this importance in an explicit manner. The Department of Enterprise, Trade and Employment's regulatory objectives are a model of clarity by comparison.

The consequences of this have been a lack of clarity in the objectives of the most important agency of financial regulation: the Central Bank. This lack of clarity in objectives has made accountability more difficult because it has been unclear what the regulatory system has been trying to achieve. This has led to a problem in assessing the effectiveness of the regulatory system but has also led to confusion about the role and responsibilities of the regulators. This was exemplified during the National Irish Bank affair in the first half of 1998 when the Central Bank was criticised for its inability to intervene on behalf of individual customers (Minutes of Evidence of the Oireachtas Committee on Finance and the Public Service, 1998: 65). It can be argued that if the objectives of the various bodies involved in financial regulation had been more explicit, the lack of a regulator with a primary consumer protection role might have been realised somewhat earlier than it was.

The government's decision to set up a new structure of financial regulation has provided an opportunity to establish more explicit policy objectives. The Central Bank and Financial Services Authority of Ireland Bill sets out the proposed functions of IFSRA as follows.

To promote the best interests of users of financial services in a way that is consistent with
a) the orderly and proper functioning of financial markets, and
b) the orderly and prudent supervision of providers of those services. (Section 33c, subsection 3).

---

[25] See http://www.entemp.ie

However, in addition to these very broad functions, the Bill proposes that

> Without limiting subsection (3), the Regulatory Authority shall take action as it considers appropriate to increase awareness among members of the public of available financial services and the costs, risks and benefits associated with the provision of those services.

This proposed function, as shall be seen in the next section, is a key objective for financial regulators in the comparator countries and is a clear change of focus for the Irish financial regulatory structure. However, the challenge is to translate these proposed functions into more focused objectives that can provide a clear framework within which the IFSRA can operate.

4.4 The policy objectives in comparison countries

The general lack of explicit policy objectives of the present structure of Irish financial regulation is in contrast with the comparator countries Britain, Australia and New Zealand. As outlined in chapter one, these countries were chosen for two reasons. The first is that they are all states with a system of governance derived from the 'Westminster' model, which allows for a meaningful comparison of their structures of political accountability. The second, and more important reason for the choice of comparators, is that Britain and Australia have both fundamentally changed their financial regulatory structures in recent years. The British government decided, in 1997, to create a single financial regulator, the Financial Services Authority (FSA), to oversee all financial institutions. Australia, in contrast, in 1998, divided responsibility for financial regulation between two authorities, with consumer regulation the responsibility of the Australian Securities and Investments Commission (ASIC) and prudential regulation the responsibility of the Australian Prudential Regulation Authority (APRA). The Reserve Bank of Australia has responsibility for the stability of the financial system. New Zealand's structure of regulation has not changed, with the Securities Commission responsible for both the efficiency and integrity of the securities markets and the Bank of New Zealand responsible for banking supervision.

However, the changes to the British and Australian regulatory structures and New Zealand's existing structure give examples of how financial regulators, and the government departments that they are accountable to, can have clear objectives. The paper does not claim that the structures of financial regulation are 'better' than in other states; comparing national structures is not a straightforward process because their responsibilities and powers usually differ in important aspects.[26] However, the paper argues that a regulatory system with clear objectives and a system of performance evaluation can, at least, be properly assessed.

4.4.1 Britain

The Treasury, as the government department responsible for the FSA, has as one of its nine objectives

> to secure an efficient market in financial services and banking with fair and efficient supervision.[27]

The FSA has in turn, four statutory objectives:

- maintaining market confidence
- promoting public awareness
- protecting consumers
- reducing financial crime.

The objectives are, in turn, clarified by six 'general duties which set out underlying principles' to which the FSA must have regard in achieving the objectives ('Objectives for a new regulator' in Financial Services Authority, 2000: 6). These are: using resources in the most economic and efficient manner; recognising the responsibilities of those who manage the affairs of authorised parties; being proportionate in imposing burdens or restrictions on the industry; facilitating innovation; taking into account the international character of financial services and the UK's competitive position; and not impeding or distorting competition unnecessarily.

4.4.2 Australia

The Department of the Treasury in Australia has overall policy and legislative responsibility for financial regulation. Financial regulation is divided between two authorities, with consumer

---

[26] See Briault (2002) for more on this.
[27] A list of the Treasury's nine objectives can be found at http://www.hm-treasury.gov.uk/About/about_aimsobject

regulation the responsibility of the Australian Securities and Investments Commission (ASIC), and prudential regulation the responsibility of the Australian Prudential Regulation Authority (APRA). The Reserve Bank of Australia has responsibility for the stability of the financial system.

The Department of the Treasury has a Financial Markets Division that describes its role as comprising

- policy advice on the structure and conduct of securities markets and investor protection in the financial sector (fundraising, takeovers, stock exchanges, futures exchanges and the regulation of financial intermediaries)
- responsibility for matters related to ASIC and for the Ministerial Council for Corporations.

The ASIC defines its role as follows:

- to protect investors, superannuants, depositors and insurance policy holders
- to regulate and enforce laws that promote honesty and fairness in financial markets, products and services and in Australian companies
- to underpin the strength, growth and international reputation of Australia's financial markets
- to maintain a public database on Australia's 1.2 million companies to provide certainty in commercial dealings
- to work with other financial, consumer and law enforcement bodies in Australia and internationally (www.asic.gov.au/about/index).

4.4.3 New Zealand
In New Zealand, the Ministry of Economic Development has legislative responsibility for the Securities Commission. The Ministry states that it 'leads the production and co-ordination of policy advice related to economic, regional and industry development' and 'is the government's primary advisor on the operation and regulation of specific markets and industries' (www.med.govt.nz/about/index). The New Zealand Securities Commission describes itself as having the fundamental purpose of fostering capital investment in New Zealand by

- promoting the efficiency of the New Zealand securities markets
- enhancing the integrity of these markets
- promoting the cost-effective regulation of these markets
- strengthening public and institutional confidence in these markets, both in New Zealand and overseas (www.sec-com.govt.nz/about/who).

The role and scope of the financial regulators in the three comparison countries differ. However, what they have in common is that their objectives are transparent and allow for a clear determination of their role as regulators. In the UK, the objectives are set out formally in legislation whereas in both Australia and New Zealand they are derived from the legislation.

4.5 Objectives of the utility regulators

The two Irish utility regulators did not have explicit policy objectives laid out in their primary legislation.[28] It was not until September 2000, when the Department of Public Enterprise (2000b) published its *Outline Legislative Proposals in Relation to the Regulation of the Communications Sector*, that formal objectives were published for the ODTR and the legislation was not enacted until April 2002. This was nearly six years after the passing of the Telecommunications (Miscellaneous Provisions) Act 1996 that established the regulator and nearly five years after the ODTR began to operate. The Communications Regulation Bill has proposed a range of objectives for the new Communications Commission, which incorporates the ODTR, that include

a) to promote competition
b) to contribute to the development of the internal market
c) to promote the interests of the users within the Community.

These broad objectives are broken down into thirteen specific sub-objectives for the different sectoral areas for which the Commission has responsibility (Communications Regulation Bill, 2002, Section 12).

---

[28] Ivan Yates, 3 February, 1999, Dáil debate on Commission for Electricity Regulation, commented that 'clearcut objectives are not set out in the Bill', and that the legislation 'also fails to set out ultimate goals'. Oireachtas Report, Dublin.

This delay in clarifying objectives was despite the Department of Public Enterprise stating as part of its 1998 Strategy Statement that 'there must be a coherent regulatory framework established by the Department', and going on to outline a set of principles that the framework should be based upon. One of the seven principles outlined was the protection of consumers. (The list of principles comprised: the protection of consumers; promotion of competition and market efficiency; equality of opportunity for market entry for all operators; price control; maintenance of service standards; consistency and predictability; and enforceability. However, the list was not included in the legislation that set up the CER in 1999 [Electricity Regulation Act, 1999]).

It could be argued that the government's seeming reluctance to set out clear policy objectives for the utility regulators in their initial legislation was caused by a conflict between its policy role as regards regulation and its ownership of the utilities.[29]

Fingleton argues that the public interest objective of utility regulation should be the maximisation of consumer welfare and there is evidence that the utility regulators have considered this to be an important objective (Fingleton, 1999: 25). The Commissioner for Energy Regulation, Tom Reeves, stated: *'the primary role of the economic regulation of natural monopolies, such as electricity transmission and distribution, is to protect the interests of consumers'* (Commission for Electricity Regulation, 1999: 3).[30] The Director of Telecommunications Regulation in her submission to the Oireachtas in April 2000 also stated:

> Simply put, my Office has one focus: that is to enable consumers to have a choice of quality telecommunications services at attractive prices. Anything that speeds and enhances this process of consumer power is to the good: anything that slows it down or gets in the way is to the bad (Director of Telecommunications Regulation, 2000).

However, such an objective was not stated explicitly until the Department of Public Enterprise published its legislative proposals in 2000. The ODTR has confirmed that the proposals, in setting out

---

[29] The government sold its stake in Eircom in June 1999 but retains ownership of the Electricity Supply Board (ESB).

[30] The Commissioner for Energy Regulation was, until Spring 2002, just the Commissioner for Electricity Regulation.

'explicitly a broad statement of objectives, fill a vacuum in the definition of the Regulator's purpose' (ODTR, September 2000, p. 1). It is beyond the scope of this paper to assess the significance of the delay in the government formulating specific policy objectives for the ODTR.[31] It is clear, however, that an organisation without clear objectives struggles to fulfil the prerequisites for political accountability.[32] The publishing of objectives for the new Communications Commission is, therefore, a welcome development.

4.6 Development of objectives for the IFSRA
The Oireachtas is the final arbiter in deciding the broad objectives for the IFSRA and will make the decision based on the CBIFSA Bill prepared by the government. This section argues that the legislative process should allow for broad discussion on the objectives and that the appropriate forum would be the Oireachtas Committee on Finance and the Public Service. Such a discussion would allow for input from both practitioners and consumers and would help to ensure that the IFSRA has legitimacy from the outset.

The UK government used such a process to allow for extensive consultation in the design of legislation that established the FSA (see Table 3).

Table 3: Timetable to set up the FSA

May 1997	Labour government announce decision to establish FSA
June 1998	FSA established
July 1998	Draft Financial Services and Markets Bill published
July-October 1998	Consultation period
November-December 1998	Treasury Select Committee
March, April, May 1999	Special Joint Committee hearings
November 1999- March 2000	Standing Committee
June 2000	Royal Assent

---

[31] There is still no equivalent setting out of objectives for the CER.
[32] The Minister for Public Enterprise described the 1996 legislation that set up the ODTR as having 'had left out the core element of accountability'. *The Irish Times*, 19 May, 2000, p. 6.

The Treasury, because of the significance of the legislation, allowed for a formal consultation period after the publication of the draft Bill. Two government committees analysed the legislation, held hearings and published reports.[33] The duplication was due to the government's decision to appoint a special joint committee to examine the legislation.

Extensive changes were made to the Bill during the legislative passage. The Treasury was criticised because of the length of the process and the extent of the changes made to the original legislation. However, the process has allowed for unprecedented debate between politicians, practitioners and consumer groups about the role of the FSA which has helped to enhance the political legitimacy of the regulator.

The initial objectives, as proposed by the Treasury, were not changed during the legislative process. There was a debate about whether the promotion of competition should be added to the four objectives but it was decided that this could lead to co-ordination problems with the Competition Commission. However, the promotion of competition remains one of the nine principles that guide the FSA in achieving its objectives.

It is clear when examining the four objectives – maintaining market confidence; promoting public awareness; protecting consumers; and reducing financial crime – that they determine the scope of the FSA's role. As Chapter 3 pointed out, the role of a financial regulator could be narrowly interpreted as objectives one and three, which would satisfy the prudential and consumer requirements. The second and fourth objectives widen the role of the FSA, reflecting the importance that the Treasury places on the two issues. ASIC in Australia has as an objective to promote the confident and informed participation of investors and consumers in the financial system; this too acts to broaden its role. It is encouraging to note that the CBIFSA Bill recommends that the IFSRA's statutory mandate should also reflect a broader role.

The objectives of both the CBIFSA and the IFSRA should be discussed at an Oireachtas Committee so that there can be a broad understanding and agreement about its role and functions. The Committee should hold hearings and call witnesses from both

---

[33] The *Financial Times* stated in an editorial that 'helpful scrutiny from two parliamentary committees has led to much rethinking by the Treasury'; 11 February, 1999, p. 18.

practitioner and consumer groups. Public hearings would also be an opportunity to discuss financial regulation in a broader context. Such a process, in a public setting, would enhance the political legitimacy and the effectiveness of the new regulatory structure.

4.7 Conclusion

This chapter highlights the fact that there is a general acceptance of the importance of policy objectives for government departments and agencies in ensuring that they are accountable. It finds that, in general, the existing Irish financial regulators have lacked explicit objectives, as have the two utility regulators. In this regard, the publication of objectives for the Communications Commission is to be welcomed.

The chapter explains that the financial regulators in the comparator countries have broad policy objectives that define their role and function. The chapter cites the example of the FSA in Britain to illustrate why discussion about policy objectives should be part of the legislative process that establishes the new regulatory structure. Such a discussion would be an important step in giving the regulator greater political legitimacy as well as helping to improve its effectiveness.

The CBIFSA Bill has proposed broad functions that provide a basis for developing policy objectives for the IFSRA. The proposal that IFSRA should take action to increase financial awareness is an important development in Irish financial regulation. However, the proposed functions must be developed into clear and concise objectives if they are to be of use.

A decision about policy objectives is also a fundamental prerequisite for accountability, because objectives determine performance. The next chapter analyses how performance can be assessed.

5

Strategy statements, work programmes and the regulators

5.1 Introduction

Chapter 4 has explained why explicit policy objectives provide the *ex ante* basis of an accountability structure for a regulator. This chapter explores how the use of accountability mechanisms such as strategy statements and work programmes can provide a means by which broad policy objectives can be translated into shorter-term targets and provide the next level in the accountability structure of the new regulator.

Strategy statements are the central part of the SMI that was given a legislative framework in the Public Service Management Act of 1997.[34] The Communications Regulation Act has required the Communications Commission to publish a bi-annual strategy statement, following the Department of Public Enterprise's proposal to extend the use of strategy statements, and an annual work programme to the utility regulators (Department of Public Enterprise, 2000a).

The chapter explores how New Zealand and Britain are using documents similar to strategy statements for regulatory agencies. It then briefly examines the lessons of departmental strategy statements and argues that for regulators, strategy statements must be part of a performance evaluation process that includes the use of indicators and targets.

5.2 The present situation for regulators

The two Irish utility regulators' relationship with the Minister of Public Enterprise was not defined in detail in their primary legislation. Both regulators are said to be independent in the conduct of their duties but the minister has responsibility for matters of policy.

---

[34] The Public Service Management Act of 1997 (Section 5[1]) has defined a strategy statement as 'comprising the key objectives, outputs and related strategies (including the use of resources) of the Department of State or Scheduled Office concerned'. Strategy statements are intended to have a three-year time frame, whereas as a work programme is intended to have only a one-year duration.

5.2.1 Strategy statements and work programmes for regulators
The Department of Public Enterprise (2000a) suggested in its March 2000 policy proposals that the utility regulators should produce strategy statements. This proposal was clarified in the Communications Regulation Act which states that

A strategy statement shall
a) be adopted within six months of the establishment day and every two years thereafter
b) take into account the objectives set out in section 12 and any directions set out in section 13 (Communications Regulation Act, 2002, section 31).

The minister also proposed that, as an annual exercise, each regulatory authority should be required

- to draw up and submit to the minister its proposed work programme (in accordance with the strategic objectives already adopted) for the following year
- to make to the minister an annual report of its activities, reviewing its performance in the previous year.

Such proposals are explicitly intended to improve the accountability structure of the utility regulators (Department of Public Enterprise, 2000a, Section 4.4). The ODTR began to publish an annual work programme at the beginning of 2000. The programme is a list of projects with intended completion dates. However, it appears that neither the ODTR nor the CER will publish a strategy statement until the proposed legislation is enacted.

The Central Bank has published one strategy statement and publishes quarterly and annual reports.[35] The Bank announced in the 2000 Annual Report that it intends to publish biannual reports 'on the current state of systemic health of the financial system in Ireland' (Central Bank of Ireland, 2001: 103). However, the Bank is not formally required to publish either a strategy statement or a work programme. The Bank's performance is subject to the C&AG's VFM appraisal process.[36] The IMF also appraised the Bank's regulatory performance in 2000 (IMF, 2001).

[35] The Central Bank's delay in publishing a further strategy statement was due to the need to await the CBIFSA legislation.
[36] The C&AG published a VFM appraisal on the Central Bank in December 1999 (Comptroller and Auditor General, 1999b).

The CBIFSA Bill proposes that IFSRA produce an annual strategic plan that must specify

- the objectives of IFSRA's activities for the financial year concerned
- the nature and scope of the activities to be undertaken
- the strategies and policies for achieving those objectives
- targets and criteria for assessing the performance of IFSRA
- the uses for which it is proposed to apply IFSRA's resources (CBIFSA Bill 2002, 33P1 and 2).

The Bill also proposes that the Consumer Director of IFSRA produces a similar strategic plan. These proposals are more comprehensive in their scope than those suggested for the utility regulators and, if fully enacted, would be a significant step in developing an accountability framework for IFSRA. However, in order for them to be effective, IFSRA must first be given overall strategic objectives.

It is clear, therefore, that work programmes, strategic plans and strategy statements are to become an important part of the accountability structure of regulators. However, it is important to clarify whether these documents have the capacity to make the desired improvement to the accountability structure.

5.2.2 Strategy statements
The Public Service Management Act (1997) has defined a strategy statement as:

comprising the key objectives, outputs and related strategies (including the use of resources) of the Department of State or Scheduled Office concerned (Public Services Management Act, 1997, Section 5(1)).

They have been described as the central part of the SMI in so far as they are intended to set out the key strategies and objectives over a three-year period (Boyle and Fleming, 2000).

The Department of the Taoiseach (1999:26) describes strategy statements as having a 'key role in the strategic management process' because 'they set out clearly the organisational goals and objectives and how to achieve them'. The Department also stresses that they 'also contribute to effective parliamentary scrutiny and are an important part of the framework of accountability.'

The first set of strategy statements was published in 1996, the second in 1998 and the third in 2001, so it should be recognised that they are still a recent development in the public service. However, a number of specific weaknesses in their implementation have been recognised that have particular relevance to the accountability structure of the utility regulators.

Figure 3: Strategic management framework

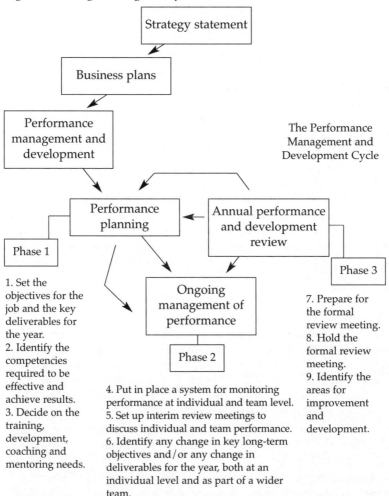

Source: Department of the Taoiseach, *Excellence through Performance,* May 2000

Boyle and Fleming (2000) have concluded in their review of strategy statements that

- there is a need for a clear link between the strategy statement and the business plan
- the annual report 'must clearly indicate both areas of progress and areas where problems have been encountered or targets not met' (Boyle and Fleming, 2000: 93)
- strategy statements must be seen as part of a *process* of strategic management.

Figure 3 underlines the validity of Boyle and Fleming's argument. Strategy statements are only the first component in the strategic management process and have limited use as stand alone documents.

The Minister for Public Enterprise intends to deal with the first of Boyle and Fleming's issues by specifying the requirement for a work programme. However, if a work programme is going to be just a list of proposed projects and documents, as indicated by the ODTR, it will have to be integrated with Boyle and Fleming's second point if it is to resemble a normal business plan.

The final point raised by Boyle and Fleming is particularly relevant to a discussion about the accountability of regulators. If a regulator produces a strategy statement without including a process of performance measurement, its significance as part of an accountability structure is limited.

5.3 Performance measurement and targets
Boyle and Fleming (2000) argue that performance measurement 'is the weakest aspect of strategy statements to date'. Keogan and McKevitt (1999) describe the performance measurement frameworks as being 'very poor' and consider that they 'lack specification and measurability'. The UK National Audit Office highlights the significance of performance measurement: it 'assists organisations to communicate objectives and priorities, measure what they deliver and report publicly on what they have achieved' (National Audit Office, 2000: 10).

The Department of the Taoiseach (1999) in a reply to Keogan and McKevitt admit that there are key challenges 'still to be addressed'. However it stresses 'it is important to remember that the framework is still being developed and is part of an evolving management process', while acknowledging that managers 'have to develop the necessary skills, competencies and *appropriate performance measures'* (Department of the Taoiseach, 1999:28 [emphasis added]).

There is evidence that it is not just in the area of strategy statements that there are concerns about measuring performance. The VFM process, undertaken by the C&AG, is an area of government where considerable attention has been placed on the development of performance indicators to measure the effectiveness of organisations. In his appraisal of the VFM studies, the C&AG has indicated that 'the overall progress in the development of improved performance reporting has been disappointing' (Comptroller and Auditor General, 1999a). These concerns were confirmed by the OECD in its recent assessment of Ireland's regulatory practices when, in commenting on the SMI, it argued that a 'lack of precise indicators and targets and an explicit auditing overview body have hampered the development of objective mechanisms of performance' (OECD, 2001: 52).

The development of performance targets for any organisation is not straightforward. Choosing targets for most activities of government does not lend itself to exact measurement and can mean the pursuit of targets to the detriment of other desirable outcomes (Osborne and Gaebler, 1993). Osborne and Gaebler outline some of the problems posed for public service management and suggest how they can be countered. They point to three particular lessons:

1   there is a difference between measuring process and measuring results
2   there is a difference between measuring efficiency and measuring effectiveness
3   there is a difference between programme outcomes and policy outcomes (Osborne and Gaebler, 1993).

These lessons are as relevant for regulators as they are for any government organisation.

5.4 Performance targets and regulators
Performance targets are an important method by which an assessment of the effectiveness of a regulator can take place. The performance targets should in theory represent a breakdown of the

objectives of the regulator into measurable and observable outcomes. Performance measurement and performance indicators are being used to assess the regulators in the comparison countries.

5.4.1 New Zealand and Britain
In New Zealand and Britain, the governments have formalised their relationship with a range of state agencies, including regulators, by introducing accountability documents that define an agency's objectives and subsequent performance for a stated period of time.

New Zealand. In New Zealand, the Securities Commission must produce both a Work Programme and a Statement of Service Performance, examples of which are outlined in Appendix 2.

The Work Programme is determined at the beginning of the year (*ex ante*) by the Securities Commission. It is divided into six categories with an estimate of the percentage of the total budget that each category will make up. The Statement of Service Performance occurs at the end of the year (*ex post*) and assesses each of the objectives of the Commission under five headings: output, quantity, quality, timeliness and cost, and outlines the activities undertaken to achieve the objectives.[37]

The Audit Office assesses the Statement of Service Performance in terms of financial accuracy while the Securities Commission comments on the outcome of each category.

The Securities Commission is an independent crown entity, established by statute, and does not therefore have to submit its work programme to the Minister for Economic Development for approval. The minister, however, tables both documents in parliament.

The advantage, from an accountability perspective, of these documents is that

1   they are based on the objectives of the Commission
2   they provide a high level of transparency for government, parliament and interested parties.

---

[37] The objectives as outlined earlier are: promoting the efficiency of the New Zealand securities markets, enhancing the integrity of these markets, promoting the cost-effective regulation of these markets and strengthening public and institutional confidence in these markets, both in New Zealand and overseas.

It could be argued that they do not provide a sufficient input for government policy into the workings of the Securities Commission but the intention in the Public Finance Act of 1989 was to ensure the independence of crown entities that have quasi-judicial responsibilities.

Crown entities that do not have quasi-judicial responsibilities have a different accountability structure. They must produce a statement of intent, which, while similar to a work programme, must be agreed by the responsible minister. The minister has the right to make changes in the statement of intent at the time of submission. However, if the minister wishes to change the policy of the crown entity at any other time, such change must be presented to parliament. This process ensures a clear division of responsibility between the minister and the crown entity.

The statement of intent for non quasi-judicial crown entities is also subject to review by the State Services Commission as well as the Audit Office. The emphasis of the State Services Commission is on the non-financial performance of the crown entity.

The State Services Commission describes its role as

> to provide assurance to the Government that the State sector has the capability, in terms of people, information, management structures and systems to deliver the Government's objectives. It also advises the Government on the performance of Public Service departments. These roles are sometimes summed up as ensuring the Government's ownership interest in the Public Service. The Commission has two main means of monitoring and assessing the state of the Government's ownership interest: the annual departmental performance assessments which it conducts, and the chief executive performance assessments which are conducted by the State Services Commissioner (New Zealand State Services website: www.ssc.government.nz).

Britain. Public Service Agreements (PSAs) were introduced in Britain in December 1998 and are broadly similar in their intent to work programmes and statements of intent in New Zealand. They are designed 'to improve both the efficiency and the accountability of government' by focusing on the results of government services (The Treasury, 1998). The Treasury extended their mandate to the utility regulators in March 1999.

A PSA describes

- the minister responsible for the PSA
- the aims and objectives of the agency/ regulator
- the resources to be allocated
- key performance targets in the delivery of its services (The Treasury, 1998).

The Treasury has described the introduction of PSAs as 'a fundamental change in the accountability of Government to Parliament and the public' (The Treasury, 1998). The Treasury is responsible for the monitoring of the achievement of the targets and reports to parliament and the public on progress in meeting the targets. When the British government announced the PSAs for the utility regulators in March 1999, performance targets were an integral part of the process.

The FSA, because it is funded by industry levy, is not subject to a PSA but produces a range of performance targets annually as part of its strategic plan. (Financial Services Authority, 2002a). It publishes three different types of measures: high-level, proxy indicators (focusing on the strategic aims and outcomes); activity-based performance results (for project work and day to day regulatory outcomes); and process measures (typically focused on the speed and efficiency of the regulatory processes). The FSA has also published a document outlining its approach to performance evaluation where it lays out in detail how measures are chosen and how the process is integrated into the management of the organisation (Financial Services Authority, 2002b).

Examples of targets that the FSA is using include

- measuring the level of company failure in financial services
- surveying financial awareness among consumers
- comparing the cost of financial regulation in Britain to other countries, using agreed benchmarks.

The FSA has also developed a model to measure the risks of not achieving its statutory objectives (Foot, 2000). The FSA appears to be taking into account Osborne and Gaebler's three lessons about the use of performance targets (see Section 5.3). It is looking to measure policy results, effectiveness and outcomes in all three of the targets.

Oftel (Office of Telecommunications), the telecommunications regulator in Britain, is subject to the PSA framework. Oftel has as its strategic aim: 'to provide the best possible deal for telecoms customers in terms of quality, choice and value for money through effective competition'. It has four outcome-based objectives to achieve this aim. For example, one of these objectives is the creation of 'well-informed consumers able to take advantage of choice'. Performance targets for this objective include

1   an increase in the proportion of consumers aware of the fact that there is a choice of supplier
2   an increase in the proportion of consumers using advanced technology
3   an increase in the proportion of consumers aware of and using price and quality comparison information provided by industry / private sector.

While there are differences in the aim and scope of the New Zealand and UK reforms, both provide for the publication of targets and an assessment of the success in meeting those targets. The publication of annual targets provides an important means by which the regulators in these countries can be held accountable by the relevant government ministry, parliament and the wider public.

5.5 Conclusion

It is encouraging to note that the CBIFSA Bill proposes that the IFSRA produces an annual strategic plan with objectives and performance targets. Such a plan, if fully implemented, would be an important step in ensuring *ex post* and *ex ante* accountability.

While the introduction of strategy statements and work programmes for the utility regulators are a significant improvement on the accountability structure that has existed, the experience of strategy statements in government departments indicates that they must not be allowed to operate in isolation.

The experience of New Zealand and the UK suggests that strategy statements and strategic plans must be part of a process that includes performance measurement and the use of performance targets if they are to be effective. The New Zealand use of *ex post* and *ex ante* accountability documents is a particularly important example of making performance transparent.

Performance indicators are not a panacea to improving either the performance or the accountability of a regulator. However, as an integral part of the process of performance evaluation, they allow for a particularly transparent mechanism for government, parliament and the public to assess a regulator's performance.

The relevant government department and Oireachtas committee can assess a regulator's performance but there is a strong argument for an agency, such as the State Services Commission in New Zealand, to provide an external appraisal of performance.

The choice of performance indicators should not be left to the IFSRA alone but agreed between the regulator, the Department of Finance and both consumers and practitioners. There should be a balance between quantitative and qualitative indicators and they should be limited in number.

The issues and concerns raised in this chapter have relevance right across the public sector. However, given the concerns about the accountability of regulators, embedding the SMI process at the outset of the new regulator would ensure

- a consistency between the broad policy objectives, the strategy statements and the work programme
- a process of performance management that would link performance targets to the short-term objectives of the work programme and the broad policy objectives.

A defined and explicit set of policy objectives is the essential basis of accountability as was discussed in the previous chapter. If this were augmented by the publication of strategy statements that are part of a process that includes true performance evaluation, concerns about the accountability of a new financial regulator could be greatly allayed.

6

Parliamentary committees and scrutiny of the IFSRA

6.1 Introduction

Democratic theory of representative government indicates that it is the role of parliament to hold the government and its agencies to account for their actions and their performance. Parliaments have, in turn, usually delegated this function to the committee system because it is more practical for a smaller group to carry out such a function. This chapter analyses the ability of the Oireachtas committee system to undertake such a role for the new financial regulator. It begins with an analysis of how the Irish committee system is increasing its powers. It then discusses the issue of resources, the experience of the Irish committee system with regulators and the committees' inquiry role.

6.2 The role of committees

Longley and Davidson (1998:1) have suggested that 'parliamentary committees have emerged as vibrant and central institutions of democratic parliaments of today's world and have begun to define new and changing roles for themselves'.

The Oireachtas committee system is showing tentative evidence of this trend. The Committee of Public Accounts inquiry into DIRT (December, 1999) is the most public manifestation of this trend,[38] but the powers of the committee system have been slowly increased over the past five years. In 1995, Oireachtas committees were given powers to draft their own legislative proposals and to hear from ministers on new legislation prior to publication. In 1997, the number and size of committees were reduced and fourteen select committees were established, each designed to shadow the work of a government department. The Compellability of Witnesses Act (1997) gave the committees the power to order witnesses to appear before them, albeit under restrictive conditions.

---

[38] See Section 2.4 for more on the DIRT inquiry.

Despite these extra powers, the relative weaknesses of the Oireachtas committee system have been well chronicled (Gallagher, 1999). These can be briefly summarised as

- governments are not keen to be scrutinised
- Oireachtas members are more interested in ministerial office than in committee work
- committee members are reluctant to criticise their party colleagues
- Oireachtas members must put constituency work first in order to assure election
- committees lack resources to conduct a scrutiny role.

These shortcomings are not all unique to the Oireachtas. The 'Westminster model' of parliament, which the Oireachtas broadly characterises, has been described as 'inherently at tension' with active parliamentary committees (Longley and Davidson, 1998: 2).

The OECD (2001: 57) has suggested that in the Irish case, 'compared to change in the executive branch, the [Irish] Parliament has been slow to assume its new regulatory accountability responsibilities'. In its ability to scrutinise an entity such as a regulator, a particularly apparent shortcoming of the Irish committee system is its lack of resources. Financial regulation can be both technical and complex and unless committee members have relevant experience to draw upon or access to the requisite expertise, a meaningful monitoring role will be very challenging.

6.3 Resources
There is general agreement that the Oireachtas committee system lacks resources. The Office of the House of the Oireachtas (1996), the OECD (2001), and O'Halpin (1998) all concur.

The lack of resources available to the Irish committee system can be characterised by comparison with those committees that monitor the financial regulators in New Zealand, Australia and Britain. Table 4 compares the resources and assumes that the Oireachtas committee that would scrutinise the IFSRA is the Joint Committee on Finance and the Public Service.

Table 4: Committee resources

	Ireland	New Zealand	Australia	United Kingdom
Committee	Finance and the Public Service	Commerce	Corporations and Securities	Treasury
Staff	1 clerk	2.5 clerks	3.5 clerks	2 clerks
Resources	Lawyer (shared with other committees)	Audit Office, advisors	Parliamentary library and specialist research staff	2 economists and advisors (part-time)

Source: Information from the staff of the four committees (2000).
Note: These are indicative figures because it is possible for committees in the Irish context to share resources. However, shared resources may lack specialist skills.

It is clear from the table that Finance and the Public Service lacks both staff and resources in comparison to its equivalent committees. The comparison with New Zealand is particularly interesting in so far as its parliament has only 120 members.

The Houses of the Oireachtas as an entity lack resources. Following research undertaken by staff of the Houses, they 'are at the bottom of the league table among EU national parliaments', according to Kieran Coughlan, Clerk to the Dáil (Committee of Public Accounts, 2000). Coughlan cites two indicators as proof of the lack of resources:

- an average of 1.2 staff per member as compared to an EU average of 2.55
- an average parliamentary budget per member of euro 0.23 million as compared to an EU average of euro 0.49 million.

Coughlan also stated that the Oireachtas library has five staff, unchanged since 1975. He compared this to Belgium that has a similar sized parliament with a library staff of forty-five. The lack of staff and, in particular, the lack of specialist expertise leads to a range of problems. The Houses of the Oireachtas have recruited a lawyer, but do not have other specialist staff with specific skills such as economics or accountancy, both of which would be required for scrutiny of a financial regulator.

The consequences of this lack of resources is, according to McDowell (2000), that politicians find themselves 'pitched into a very unequal battle with the well-resourced, well-researched Executive arm of the State'. A financial regulator such as ISFRA will also have access to considerable expertise. McDowell's view has been confirmed during the interview process where the example was given of briefing notes having being prepared for committee members by the government department that was to be questioned. Gallagher suggests that the lack of resources has also led to committees becoming 'captives of interest groups supplying apparently plausible arguments and data' (Gallagher, 1999: 198). The lack of staff is accentuated by the small size of the budget that each committee has at its disposal, amounting to approximately €25,000 on an annual basis. This greatly restricts the ability of a committee to hire advisors or consultants to carry out specific research projects.

The government, in its November 2000 document, *A New Dáil for a New Millennium,* announced a series of measures designed to strengthen the role of the committee system. The document adopted a proposal of the Public Accounts Committee that an Oireachtas commission be established with a separate Vote so that the committee system is no longer dependent on the executive for its day-to-day funding. The document also suggested that the Dáil should devote one week per month to meeting only in committee (Brennan, 2000). It also proposed that the Vote be increased substantially. Couglan argues that to increase the level of resources to the EU average would require an increase in the annual budget of 110 per cent to €109 million (Coughlan, Committee of Public Accounts, 2000).

Under the current system, it appears that the Committee of Finance and the Public Service could be, in part, dependent for its funding on the very government department that has policy responsibility for the ISFRA.

6.4 The role of the C&AG within the committee system

The comparator countries chosen for this study, New Zealand and the UK, offer an example of how the Irish committee system could strengthen its oversight role by use of the C&AG's powers of inquiry. In Ireland, the Committee of Public Accounts is the only committee that is provided with the reports of the C&AG.

The Audit Office in New Zealand and the UK perform a broadly similar role to that of the C&AG in Ireland. However, in both these countries, all the parliamentary committees can use the reports of the Audit Office and, in certain circumstances, request the Office to conduct specific inquiries.

Audit Office advisers regularly advise committees on Estimates and financial reviews, providing analysis of budgets and performance of government departments. The Audit Office can provide advice on inquiries committees establish and it can undertake investigations and report back to the committee (Office of the Clerk of the House of Representatives of New Zealand, 2000: 23).

In the UK, parliamentary committees consult the National Audit Office (NAO) on specific issues and the committees use the NAO's published research. The General Accounting Office (GAO) in the United States performs a similar role, 'carrying out a large number of performance auditing projects and programme evaluations' (OECD, 1997b: 110). The GAO carries out such functions for all congressional committees.

The Oireachtas committees could benefit from these examples, using both the information in the C&AG's existing reports and also commissioning specific reports. The Reports on Evaluation of Effectiveness of individual government institutions (known as the VFM studies) could be of significant value to the committees in their 'scrutiny' role. These are intended to provide independent assurance to Dáil Eireann on the discharge by entities audited by the C&AG of their accountability for

- the economic and efficient use of public moneys and other resources
- the effectiveness of their operations.

The VFM reports could provide an excellent basis for committees to pursue their own research agenda. The report on Central Bank Financial Regulation, published in December 1999, was the first public assessment of the regulatory effectiveness of the Bank (Comptroller and Auditor General, 1999b). If the examples of the comparator countries were followed, it could provide an excellent basis for further analysis for the Committee on Finance and the Public Service.

If the C&AG were asked to assist other committees, the office would require greater resources. It would also be important not to compromise the independence of the C&AG's office. However, given the experience of New Zealand, Britain and the United States, it appears that the issue of independence can be managed.

6.5 The committee system and the regulators
The relationship between the utility regulators and the Oireachtas committee system had an unfortunate beginning when the Director of Telecommunications Regulation declined an invitation to appear before the Joint Committee on Public Enterprise and Transport in January 1998.

The Director stated in her response to the Committee that 'by virtue of the Telecommunications (Miscellaneous Provisions) Act 1996 which created the Office of Telecommunications Regulation I am independently responsible as regulator of telecommunications and my office does not therefore fall within the remit of the Joint Committee' (Report of the Joint Committee on Public Enterprise and Transport, 1998). The joint committee promptly altered its Orders of Reference to include a specific reference to 'such public affairs administered by the Director of Telecommunications Regulation as it may select'. The Director subsequently appeared in front of the Joint Committee in February 1998 and has subsequently appeared each time requested.

The Minister of State responsible for the legislation described the affair subsequently:

> I tried to ensure accountability and to reduce the democratic deficit in that Act, but the Act fell in that regard at the very first fence when the director of telecommunications regulation refused to attend the Committee on Public Enterprise and Transport (Stagg, 1999).

The Department of Public Enterprise (2000a) has stressed the importance of the regulators appearing before the Oireachtas. The legislation that established the CER, the Commission for Aviation Regulation and the Communications Commission has made provision for attendance at Oireachtas committees

From time to time, and whenever so requested, the Commission shall account for the performance of its functions to a Joint Committee of the Oireachtas and shall have regard to any recommendations of such Joint Committee relevant to its function (Aviation Regulation Bill 2000, Section 27 (3)).

However, the Oireachtas has shown little enthusiasm in carrying out its scrutiny role. The Director of Telecommunication Regulation has appeared in front of the Committee on Public Enterprise and Transport on only three occasions since 1998, with the last meeting occurring in April 2000. The CER has appeared only once in front of an Oireachtas committee since the commission commenced operation in September 1999.

The Governor of the Central Bank first appeared in front of an Oireachtas committee in March 1995, having indicated a willingness to do so when he was appointed in 1994. This was a change in approach from the bank, a governor never having previously appeared in front of an Oireachtas committee.

The Governor has appeared in front of five different committees since 1995. These are detailed in Table 5.

Table 5: Central Bank Governor's meetings with Oireachtas committees (1995-2001)

Committee	Appearance
Finance and General Affairs	28 March 1995
	13 September 1995
	8 March 1996
	3 July 1996
Finance and Public Service	18 February 1998
	1 April 1998
	13 October 1999
	18 July 2001
	7 November 2001
Enterprise and Economic Strategy	8 January 1997
Committee on European Affairs	3 June 1998
	23 February 2000
	19 July 2000
	22 February 2001

Committee	Appearance
Committee of Public Accounts	15 October 1998 1 September 1999 20 June 2000 11 July 2000 28 November 2000 7 March 2001

Source: Various Central Bank Annual Reports. (It should be noted that the Finance and the Public Service Committee replaced the Finance and General Affairs Committee.)

The range of committees reflects the extent of the role of the Central Bank. The Committee on Finance and the Public Service (and its predecessor, Finance and General Affairs) is the natural committee to hold the Central Bank to account. However, it is interesting to note that three of the Governor's meetings with the Committee on Finance and the Public Service focused on particular regulatory controversies rather than on the need to account for the activities and performance of the bank. It is also interesting to note the lack of a regular schedule with the Governor not appearing before the Finance and the Public Service Committee in 2000, resulting in a twenty-month gap in his appearances.

The apparent unwillingness of different Oireachtas committees to meet with the different regulators on even an annual basis is an indication of a reluctance to take seriously a scrutiny role.

A number of interviewees commented on the experience of appearing before an Oireachtas committee. They remarked on the disparity in the knowledge of committee members and the tendency to move away from policy issues to focus on matters of constituency concern. There was also mention of committee members' inability to remain present for an entire meeting and the frequency of late arrival and early departure.

The CBIFSA Bill has proposed that the chairperson, the chief executive and the consumer director of IFSRA should be available to an Oireachtas committee if requested to appear (CBIFSA Bill 2002, section 33AM). The appropriate committee to monitor the IFSRA remains the Joint Committee on Finance and the Public Service, but it is important that a regular schedule is adhered to, preferably after the publication of its annual report. This would not preclude the committee from calling the regulator to account on other occasions. However, it would allow for a formal discussion about the performance of the IFSRA rather than a focus on a specific issue as has happened with meetings with the Governor of the Central Bank.

This is the norm in Australia, New Zealand and the UK where the financial regulator comes before the relevant committee at least once a year and at other times if requested.

6.6 Inquiry role

In the area of financial regulation there have been two Oireachtas committee reports that have held inquiries which subsequently recommended major changes to the system. The first was the Joint Committee on Enterprise and Economic Strategy (1997c) that recommended the establishment of a single regulator in April 1997. The second report was the Joint Committee on Finance and the Public Sector (1998b) that recommended the setting-up of a single regulatory authority in July 1998. Both committees held hearings and the Committee on Finance and the Public Service travelled to a range of European countries to investigate their regulatory regimes.

The government, in laying down the brief for the Implementation Advisory Group, adopted the Committee on Finance and the Public Service's recommendation that a single regulatory agency be established.

The Oireachtas committee system has, because of its limited resources, had a limited role in producing reports on specific issues. The Public Accounts Committee (PAC) has suggested a range of measures designed to strengthen the inquiry role. The DIRT report by the PAC, published in December 1999, has raised the profile and the expectations of what an Oireachtas committee can achieve in an inquiry in terms of ensuring democratic accountability (Committee of Public Accounts, 1999). However, it would be misleading to draw too many comparisons between the PAC report and the normal Oireachtas committee inquiry. The PAC sub-committee had the C&AG's report to use as a basis of its inquiry. It is estimated that the sub-committee spent approximately €1.28 million, or three times the annual research budget of the entire committee system. This gave the sub-committee access to high-level legal and accounting expertise. The work of other Oireachtas committees was severely restricted over the period because of the demand that the sub-committee placed on the resources of the Oireachtas.[39]

However, the Committee on Finance and the Public Service's report of July 1998 is an indication that Oireachtas committees can have a significant input into government policy on financial regulation.

Table 6: List of reports laid by the Committee on Finance and the Public Service between November 1997 and May 2000

- Work programme 1998
- Interim Report: report on review of banking policy: the regulation and supervision of financial institutions
- Interim Report: report on review of banking policy: the regulation and supervision of financial institutions: minutes of evidence of 1 April and 22 April 1998
- Final Report: report on review of banking policy: the regulation and supervision of financial institutions
- Annual report 1998
- Report of the Department of Finance statement of strategy 1998-2000
- Report on the Government proposals for a Standards in Public Office Bill
- Work programme 1999
- Report on proposals for a prevention of corruption Bill
- Annual report of the Joint Committee on Finance and the public Service (1999)
- Report of meeting on report of the Implementation Advisory Group on the establishment of a single regulatory authority for the financial services sector.
- Work Programme 2000 *Source:* Joint Oireachtas Committee on Finance and the Public Service

---

[39] The inquiry role of Oireachtas committees has been limited by the Supreme Court ruling in April 2002 following a legal challenge to the Joint Committee on Justice, Equality and Women's Rights concerning the inquiry into the shooting dead by gardaí of John Carthy at Abbeylara, Co Longford. The court stopped the Abbeylara inquiry on grounds of how the inquiry was being conducted. This highlights the importance of getting procedural and operational matters of Oireachtas inquiries clear and precise.

It is interesting to analyse the list of reports prepared by the Committee between November 1997 and May 2000. The Committee produced twelve reports (Table 6). If the work programmes, annual reports and reports on meetings are removed from the list, the number of researched reports is as few as three. (Taking the two interim reports and one final report on financial regulation as a single report.) This contrasts with the UK Treasury Committee which between May 1997 and December 1999 produced eighteen reports.[40]

If the Committee had access to greater resources and expertise, the inquiry role could play a more significant role in holding agencies such as IFSRA to account.

6.7 Legislative role

The committee system has a defined role under standing orders in the preparation of legislation. The appropriate committee takes the third stage of legislation and amendments can be proposed 'provided they do not conflict with the principles of the Bill, since this was approved by the house at the second stage' (Gallagher, 1999: 185). Committees have also had, since 1995, the ability to initiate legislation although it appears to have been used sparingly.

For legislation as important as the establishment of a new financial regulator, there is a strong argument for the Committee on Finance and the Public Service to hold formal hearings after the initial publication of the legislation. This would give practitioners, consumer groups and other interested parties the opportunity to comment in public, and allow the committee to amend the legislation as appropriate.

In the UK, the legislative process setting up the FSA debated over 2,000 amendments and parliament made some significant changes to the legislation as a result. An example of the significance of the changes was the amendment that gave the consumer panel a statutory basis.

A further potential role for the committee system is as a forum for confirmation hearings of appointees to specific offices. This is the practice in the United States where senior appointments to government agencies and regulators must come before the appropriate Senate committee to seek ratification of their

---

[40] Information supplied by the Clerk of UK Treasury Committee.

appointment. This gives the committee the opportunity to question the candidates about their views and their relevant experience. Laver has suggested that a reformed Seanad could play a role in this process (Laver, 1996). Confirmation hearings could be used for board appointments to IFSRA.

6.8 The political will

Gallagher outlines a series of reasons why the committee system has not assumed a strong scrutiny role in the political process and concludes that a powerful factor is the fact that government deputies perceive their main role as supporting the government (Gallagher, 1999). He also argues that TDs are, not surprisingly, more interested in re-election than committee work.

The evidence of the committee system at work in its scrutiny of regulators does little to dispute Gallagher's argument. The comments from interviewees about the disparity in the preparation of members, and the inability of members to attend entire meetings appear to confirm a relative lack of interest. There also appears to be no discernable timetable in calling regulators to appear before their 'marking' committee. The non-appearance of the Central Bank Governor before the Finance and Public Service Committee for twenty months between October 1999 and July 2001 and the Director of Telecommunications Regulation before the Public Enterprise and Transport Committee between April 2000 and April 2002 confirm this lack of timetable.

It cannot be concluded, therefore, that a decision to increase the resources available to the committee system or a decision to devote one week every month that the Dáil is sitting to committees will result in a consequential increase in their effectiveness as scrutinisers of the regulators. This will be dependent on a change of attitude among TDs about the significance of the work.[41]

The evidence in other states is that committees are increasing their legislative and scrutiny roles. This role appears to be evolving particularly slowly in the Oireachtas.

6.9 Conclusion

The committee system as it is presently constituted will struggle to fulfil its mandate to hold the regulator to account. The system is

---

[41] Verheijen and Millar (1998: 114) state that as well as extra resources, a strengthened committee system needs 'a change in mentality from Irish TDs'.

clearly under-resourced and therefore lacks access to expertise to question the financial regulator or indeed any other regulator about its performance. The apparent unwillingness of committees to meet with the different regulators on even an annual basis is an indication that the scrutiny role is not a serious priority.

The chapter suggests that the committee system could examine the example of New Zealand in using its Audit Office as an extra resource for its scrutiny role. However, the Committee on Finance and the Public Service clearly requires access to specialist skills if it is to perform a meaningful monitoring role.

The chapter suggests that there is evidence of a lack of a political will to use the committee system to scrutinise regulatory authorities as indicated by the long gaps between meetings.

The Department of the Taoiseach's proposals to create an Oireachtas commission and to commit one week per month to committees is an encouraging step. The real test of 'political will' will happen when the system is properly resourced. Until that occurs, the committee system will struggle to fulfil its democratic mandate to hold the IFSRA to account.

7

Citizen accountability

7.1 Introduction

The Department of Finance concurred with the McDowell Report when it proposed 'the establishment of two panels representative of consumer and industry interests' and suggested that they would provide 'fora for discussions on the performance of the regulator in carrying out its regulatory duties as well as providing opportunities for the industry and consumer interests to suggest initiatives which they wish to see pursued' (McDowell Report, 1999: 37). The statutory requirement for a regulator to have consumer and practitioner panels will be a first for the Irish regulatory system. However, the requirement was not contained in the CBIFSA Bill, but according to the Department of Finance, will be contained in a second piece of financial regulation legislation.

This chapter analyses *ex post* mechanisms that are designed to enhance the level of direct citizen participation in the accountability structure. It argues that establishing a well-resourced consumer panel should be the most important of these mechanisms but that there are other means that should also be considered by the ISFRA.[42]

7.2 Panels in the comparison countries

Consumer panels have been part of the accountability structures of the regulators in the comparator countries since they were established. In the UK, the FSA is required by statute to establish and maintain a consumer panel. It describes itself and its role as follows

> We were established by the Financial Services Authority (FSA) in December 1998 to provide advice on the interests and concerns of consumers and to assess the FSA's effectiveness in meeting its objectives to protect consumers' interests and promote public

---

[42] The paper does not analyse the potential role of the financial services ombudsman or the legal appeals mechanisms.

understanding of the financial system' (Financial Services Authority website).[43]

The aims of the panel are

- to influence FSA policy
- to influence government policy and legislation
- to understand consumer needs by commissioning research and discussion papers
- to keep in touch with consumer representatives and trade associations.

The panel, while funded by the FSA, describes itself as independent and produces research and policy recommendations for both the FSA and the government. The 2000 Annual Report of the panel states that it published nineteen reports, commissioned three research papers, two working papers and addressed thirty-two different areas where the FSA sought the panel's advice (Consumer Panel of the FSA, 2000).

In Australia, ASIC has also established a consumer panel. It describes itself as 'an active advisory panel that allows consumers to comment on our proposed policies'. Furthermore it states that it encourages consumers to identify issues that directly affect them and has been given the resources to research those issues (Australian Securities and Investment Commission website).[44]

The FSA and ASIC both have practitioner panels that have objectives and aims similar to the consumer panels. The FSA panels produce annual and specific reports highlighting issues of concern to which the board of the FSA must respond.

Oftel, the British equivalent to the ODTR, has statutory bodies known as advisory committees that play a similar role to consumer and practitioner panels that

carry out a range of activities: consumer research, monitoring of complaints trends, consultation with other consumer organisations, telecoms companies and government departments, running conferences, responding to Oftel and government consultation papers, and publishing occasional information leaflets. Each committee publishes an annual report and consults annually on its future plans (Oftel Consumer Panel website).[45]

---

[43] See http://www.fsa.government.uk
[44] See http://www.asic.government.au
[45] See http://www.oftel.gov.uk

Assessing the effectiveness of the panels in meeting their objectives is not straightforward. However, they do provide a mechanism by which consumers' views can be aggregated and represented to both the regulator and to the government. Such a process is an important counterweight to the strength of producer lobbies in regulatory debates.

7.3 Consumer panels in Ireland

In Ireland, the establishment of a consumer panel for the IFSRA will not be straightforward because there is not a tradition of a strong consumer lobby in Ireland.[46] The OECD (2001) commented that 'consumer interests are not well represented in policy debate and deliberation in Ireland, which remains dominated by producer interests'. (OECD, 2001: 105). The consumer panel will, therefore, have to be chosen carefully, comprising citizens with experience and understanding of the complex issues involved in the regulatory process. By contrast, there is a wide range of practitioner bodies to represent the financial services industry.

It is important that the consumer panel has its own research budget and that, as with the FSA in the UK, the IFSRA must formally respond to its policy recommendations. The Communications Regulation Bill that has set up the Communications Commission has not provided a statutory role for either consumer or practitioner panels.[47] This is surprising given the OECD's recent comments, the prevalence of panels in other states with similar regulatory structures and recent comments from both the Minister of Public Enterprise and the Taoiseach. The Minister for Public Enterprise suggested in her March 2000 policy proposals the need for measures to protect the customer interests (Department of Public Enterprise, 2000a). The Taoiseach, when announcing the establishment of the National Regulatory Review, acknowledged the OECD Report and emphasised that the government is keen to find a greater role for consumer groups in the drafting of regulatory legislation (Ahern, *The Irish Times*, 28 February, 2002, p. 18). The lack of a statutory consumer panel will make it very difficult to give consumers a meaningful role in the regulatory process.

---

[46] The OECD (2001: 105) comments that there are no consumer groups among the forty bodies identified as participants in the negotiations of the social partners' Programme for Prosperity and Fairness.
[47] The ODTR has had no formal panels but established a consumer forum in May 2000 which meets formally with the regulator twice a year.

7.4 Other direct mechanisms
There are other methods for regulators to interact with practitioners and consumers.

7.4.1 Town meetings
Financial regulators such as the FSA, ASIC and particularly the Securities and Exchange Commission (SEC) in the United States all hold regular town meetings. The object of such meetings is to allow an audience of 'ordinary citizens' to question the regulator (usually the chairperson) while also allowing the regulator to find out the issues that concern the public. Such meetings allow the regulator to speak directly to investors.

The former chairman of the SEC, Arthur Levitt, held forty-two town meetings during the eight years of his tenure between 1993 and 2001 (Levitt, 2001).

7.4.2 Technology
The increasing level of Internet penetration is an opportunity for regulators to interact with consumers in a range of ways. Financial regulators in the comparator countries are using their websites to provide a range of investment information in a manner that is accessible to the public. Such information is not currently available to the Irish public.

The FSA in the UK also uses a telephone call service for consumers with complaints or enquiries.

7.4.3 Customer service programmes
The introduction of the Quality Customer Service Initiative has led to the establishment of customer service programmes (Humphreys, 1998). The Department of Social, Community and Family Affairs (renamed the Department of Social and Family Affairs in June 2002), for example, has set up a range of customer panels drawn at random from its customer lists and uses them to discuss issues ranging from payment methods to access for people with disabilities. Panels have been set up for customer groups such as the unemployed, older people and carers. The Department states that 'CPs [Customer Plans] are established so that various categories of our customers can meet our staff to express their needs and concerns' (Department of Social, Community and Family Affairs, 1998).

The findings from the panels are used in the relevant policy area and specific decisions are reported back to the panels. The department also uses professional surveys outside its offices around the country as another means of gaining feedback. The department also operates a business users' panel jointly with the Revenue Commissioners to obtain feedback from the business community.

There are, therefore, different ways of interacting with people that utilise the services of a regulator. The practitioner and consumer panels allow for direct input into the deliberations of a regulator. The survey approach as undertaken by the Department of Social, Community and Family Affairs would ensure that a regulator such as IFSRA has feedback directly from the public on how it is meeting its objectives.

7.5 Financial awareness in Ireland

There is a general perception that the level of financial awareness in Ireland is low. 'Consumer awareness of, and education on, financial matters is minimal' (Irish Association of Investment Managers, 1998). This situation is not surprising given the lack of education about the issue.

This is not a problem unique to Ireland. The chairman of the FSA has described the problem of investors in Britain wanting to purchase financial products but finding that 'their financial understanding does not match the standard needed to be able to find one's way through a maze of competing products, often of great complexity' (Davies, 2000). The FSA has carried out a range of consumer surveys that have confirmed a low level of knowledge about financial products (FSA, 2000).

In Britain and Australia the financial regulators have been given a statutory objective to raise the level of financial awareness. It should be welcomed that the CBIFSA Bill proposes that IFSRA should have a similar role in Ireland. The need to raise the level of financial awareness is given even greater urgency by the increase in defined contribution pension funds where the investment risk falls on the individual rather than the company (see Appendix 1 for a discussion of the pension issue).

7.5.1 Financial education in Ireland

There is no mandatory second level course that teaches school students about basic financial concepts such as banking, insurance or pensions. The Junior Certificate level course in Civic, Social and Political Education, which is mandatory and has the stated aim of developing 'active citizens' that have 'a capacity to gain access to information and structures', does not have a module that deals with financial awareness.[48] The Department of Education in Britain has recently announced its intention of including personal finance in its Personal, Social and Health Education course at secondary level. Lobbying from the Personal Finance Educational Group (a pressure group funded by both financial services groups and the FSA) preceded this decision.

7.5.2 Role of regulators

As stated, the FSA in Britain has been given as one of its four broad policy objectives that of 'promoting public awareness'. The organisation has committed itself to pursuing two main aims under this objective:

- to improve general financial literacy
- to improve the information and advice available to consumers.

The FSA has established a specific consumer unit to help to promote these aims.

In Australia, ASIC has an objective to 'promote the confident and informed participation of investors and consumers in the financial system'. ASIC also undertakes a range of measures by which it pursues this objective with information and warnings about investment products.

In the United States, the SEC also undertakes an educational role. It carries out a range of educational functions and participates in the Alliance for Investor Education. This alliance 'is dedicated to facilitating greater understanding of investing, investments and the financial markets among current and prospective investors of all ages'. It 'pursues initiatives for education and joins with others to motivate Americans to obtain objective information and increase their knowledge and understanding of markets' (Alliance for Investor Education website).[49]

---

[48] Quoted in National Council for Curriculum and Assessment (1999). However, an estimated 45,000 students (out of a total of 60,000) undertake a business studies course at Junior Certificate level, according to Department of Education estimates.
[49] See http://www.investoreducation.org

As described, all three regulators use a range of mechanisms by which they pursue their objective of educating the public about personal finance, with particular use of websites to provide easily accessible information.

Ireland, with its splintered financial regulatory framework, has lacked one regulator with responsibility for consumer protection. This, in turn, has meant that there has been no regulator or government agency that has perceived itself as having responsibility for informing and educating the public. The proposal that IFSRA should undertake this role is, therefore, to be welcomed.

7.6 Conclusion

The government's proposal that the IFSRA should have both a practitioner and a consumer panel is consistent with the normal practice of both financial and utility regulators internationally and should be welcomed. The IFSRA consumer panel should have its own independent research budget and IFSRA should be mandated to reply formally to its findings.

There has been no statutory requirement for the utility regulators to have panels. The utility regulators have constant interaction with the practitioners but have struggled to interact with consumers. The lack of a well-developed consumer lobby in Ireland has made the consultative process more difficult than it appears to be in other countries. The recognition by the government of the problems posed by the lack of such a lobby, in the launch of the consultative process designed to review regulatory standards, is an important step. However, the lack of a statutory position for a consumer panel in the legislation to establish the Communications Commission is at variance with the government's concern. The government should consider how it could assist in the creation of consumer groups so that they could play a meaningful role in the regulatory process.

The decision that IFSRA should be given a statutory objective of raising the level of financial awareness is to be welcomed. It has the opportunity to study best practices among regulators in other countries and initiate a programme to pursue the objective. The longer-term strategy to raise financial awareness should include financial education becoming part of the school curriculum from an early stage. There is a definite need for a mandatory course at Junior Certificate level to educate children about the basic concepts to ensure financial literacy. The experience of the Personal Finance Education Group in the UK can be called upon.

However, the IFSRA should be given the responsibility of ensuring that all citizens can access information designed to improve their understanding. The IFSRA should utilise direct means of communication with the public such as town meetings, the use of technology and direct consumers surveys as an important part of fulfilling their educational objective.

8

Conclusions

The primary aim of this paper has been to assess the accountability structure for the IFSRA, the proposed new single financial regulator. The challenge in designing such a structure is emphasised by the need for the regulator to be independent of the political process in respect of its specific rule-making and adjudicative functions. The paper contends that an accountability structure with appropriate *ex ante* and *ex post* mechanisms can ensure that the financial regulator maintains the appropriate balance between independence and accountability. While the design of such mechanisms is not straightforward, the paper asserts that they minimise the risk of a regulator assuming unaccountable authority, the risk of political interference in the regulatory process, and the potential for regulatory capture.

Before discussing the accountability mechanisms, the paper reviewed the requirement for financial regulation and the existing structure of financial regulation in Ireland. It stated that there are two assumptions that underlie the need for financial regulation: the concepts of systemic risk, and asymmetric information. It argued that the evolution of financial regulation, with no one government department responsible for policy, led to an emphasis on avoiding systemic risk rather than developing policies to counter asymmetric information. This emphasis led to the realisation that a 'consumer gap' existed in the regulatory structure and the subsequent government decision to create a single regulatory authority.

However, the government's decision not to accept the McDowell Report's recommendation that the new regulator should be a 'stand-alone' body has important implications for the IFSRA's accountability structure. In particular, the decision that the Governor of the Central Bank should be the chair of the CBIFSA implies that a key member of the new regulatory structure will not be removable from office by the government or the Oireachtas. The paper asserts that these decisions mean that despite the legislation's attempts to outline the duties and responsibilities of the IFSRA, there remain significant doubts about the new regulator's operational independence and considerable scope for confusion about lines of responsibility and accountability.

The analysis of the accountability mechanisms was divided into three parts:

1   the objectives of the regulator
2   measuring the performance of the regulator
3   the methods by which it is to be scrutinised.

The study has argued that clear and concise policy objectives are the basis of an accountability structure because they determine the functions that the state is delegating to the regulator. If the objectives of the regulator are not clarified, its role is unclear, thereby lessening its legitimacy as an institution of governance.

The other role that objectives play in the accountability structure is to allow for measurement of performance. If the government is not clear what functions it is asking the IFSRA to undertake, it will not be possible to assess its performance.

The paper finds that the objectives of the Central Bank as a financial regulator and the ODTR as a utility regulator have not been explicitly stated.[50] This has led to confusion about their roles and responsibilities that has damaged their political legitimacy. This has also made an assessment of their performance difficult.

This lack of clear objectives has been contrasted with those of financial regulators in the comparison countries. While the paper welcomes the CBIFSA Bill's proposal that IFSRA should be given a statutory responsibility of raising financial awareness, it argues that given the importance of financial regulation, there should be wide consultation on the objectives for the IFSRA. Such consultation would be an important step in giving the regulator both greater political legitimacy as well as helping to improve its ultimate effectiveness.

However, the paper argues that at the end of the consultation period, IFSRA must be given clear and succinct objectives if it is to succeed both as a regulator and be accountable to the political system.

The paper welcomes the proposal that IFSRA should publish an annual strategic plan. It argues that the lack of such planning for the

---

[50] The study has focused on the ODTR rather than the CER because the CER has been in existence for a very short period.

existing system of financial regulation and the utility regulators has proven to be a major flaw in their structure of accountability. However, if the strategic planning is to be effective, it must be part of a process that includes performance evaluation and the use of performance targets. This has been recognised as a weakness in the use of strategy statements by government departments (see Boyle and Fleming, 2000). The example of New Zealand is cited where both *ex post* and *ex ante* accountability documents are published so the performance of a regulatory agency can be assessed on an annual basis.

The combination of explicit policy objectives and a strategic plan that is part of a performance evaluation process can provide the basis for an accountability structure where the role of the ISFRA is defined and its performance can be assessed.

The second part of the accountability structure for the SRA to be considered in the paper was *the mechanisms by which it is to be scrutinised.*

These were assessed under three headings

1   Oireachtas committees
2   Consumer and Practitioner Panels
3   Public consultation.

The paper concluded that the Oireachtas committee system's lack of resources combined with an apparent lack of political will could limit its ability to hold a regulator such as the IFSRA to account. The study suggests that the reports of the C&AG could be used to augment the resources of the committees in their scrutiny role as the New Zealand committee system uses the work of the Audit Office. The paper also argued that the Oireachtas Committee on Finance and the Public Service should conduct public hearings to discuss the objectives for IFSRA, as occurred in Britain, when the House of Commons held hearings as part of the consultative process in designing the legislation establishing the FSA. Such hearings would provide a forum for public debate about the role and objectives of financial regulation in Ireland.

The Oireachtas committee system's relationship with regulators had a difficult start when the ODTR initially refused a request to appear.[51] The primary legislation establishing both the CER and the

---

[51] The Governor of the Central Bank did not appear in front of an Oireachtas committee until 1995.

Commission for Aviation Regulation has clarified their obligation to appear as requested. However, the inability of Oireachtas committees to meet with regulators on even an annual basis is an indication that a scrutiny role is not yet being taken seriously. The paper has argued that the Oireachtas and its committees should be the pre-eminent mechanism by which the SRA should be held to account. However, its apparent limitations have increased the importance of other mechanisms of accountability.

The government's proposal that the IFSRA should have both practitioner and consumer panels is consistent with the normal practice of both financial and utility regulators internationally. The IFSRA consumer panel should have its own independent research budget and the IFSRA should be mandated to reply formally to their findings.

The paper has examined how the public could have *direct* interaction with the IFSRA as well as being represented through consumer groups. The use of town meetings, customer surveys and websites as media of direct communication was examined. These methods are all being utilised with apparent success by financial regulators in Australia, Britain, New Zealand and the United States.

The ultimate objective of the IFSRA's direct interaction with the public should be to raise the level of public awareness about financial matters. The paper welcomes the proposal in the CBIFSA legislation that this should be a policy objective for the IFSRA and suggests that it should be given the responsibility of ensuring that all citizens can access information designed to improve their financial awareness.

The paper has not analysed the IFSRA's relationship with the Competition Authority or the proposed methods of legal appeal. The IFSRA's concerns about competition will be different to that of the ODTR, which has in the past come into direct jurisdictional conflict with the Competition Authority, but it is important that responsibility is defined in the IFSRA's enabling legislation. The right to appeal decisions to the courts has also caused a problem for the ODTR. The McDowell Report has suggested in some detail how this issue can be resolved for the SRA and it is likely that the IFSRA can adopt similar proposals.

A summary of the main policy proposals is that

- clear and concise policy objectives are defined for the IFSRA

- the IFSRA publish a strategic plan
- performance evaluation and performance targets be part of the planning process
- the Oireachtas committee system is given access to more resources to allow it to carry out its scrutiny role. However, the paper recognises that without a greater level of political commitment, extra resources will not guarantee a more sophisticated level of scrutiny
- the consumer and practitioner panels are given statutory recognition, research budgets and that the IFSRA must formally respond to their proposals
- the IFSRA utilises innovative methods to interact directly with the public
- the IFRSA should be given the formal objective of raising the level of financial awareness
- the IFSRA be subject to a regular external review to assess its performance.

The political system's experience with the utility regulators and, in particular, the ODTR has not been a particularly happy one.[52] The ODTR's initial legislation failed to lay out an accountability framework. It did not determine objectives, or any rigorous account of performance. Its interaction with the Competition Authority and the legal system was not defined satisfactorily at the outset. It was not mandated to report to the Oireachtas or to establish a consumer panel. The Minister for Public Enterprise has proposed and enacted various measures to improve its accountability structure. Some of these proposals have been implemented in the legislation that has established the CER and the Commission for Aviation Regulation. It was only the enactment of the Communications Regulation legislation in the spring of 2002 and the creation of the Communication Commission that has seen some of these problems rectified. However, the decision not to allow for the statutory provision of consumer and practitioner panels is very surprising given the OECD's recent comments about the lack of consumer representation in the Irish regulatory process and the Taoiseach's acknowledgement of the problem.

---

[52] The Minister for Public Enterprise stated that the 1996 legislation that set up the ODTR 'had left out the core element of accountability', *The Irish Times*, 19 May, 2000.

The CBIFSA legislation that sets up the IFSRA appears to have addressed many of the problems with the accountability structure of the ODTR. However, the government's decision not to follow the recommendation of the McDowell Report to establish IFSRA as a new and stand-alone regulator, but to give the Governor of the Central Bank as the chair of CBIFSA a role at the apex of the new regulatory structure, increases the need to define clearly the IFSRA's objectives and role so as to ensure its independence.

It is also important to realise that emphasis must be placed on the entire structure of accountability. Defining objectives and measuring performance is of limited value if it cannot be scrutinised effectively. There remains a great onus on the Oireachtas to improve its performance in this regard.

In a sense, the problems with the accountability of regulators reflect a wider problem of the accountability of the entire public service. However, given the particular role the state has delegated to regulators such as the IFSRA, designing an accountability structure is a measure of the capacity of the political process to come to terms with new methods of governance. Given the importance of proper regulation of financial services, there could be a high cost to the state of not getting it right from the outset.

Appendix 1

This appendix explains why there is a need to raise the level of financial awareness.

Change in pension provision

There has been a major change in the provision of pensions in Ireland over the past five years.

The growth in defined contribution schemes

The major change in pension fund provision from defined benefit to defined contribution schemes is indicated in Table A1.

A defined contribution pension is one where the individual is responsible for accumulating sufficient assets with which to fund a retirement income. This contrasts with a defined benefits pension where an individual is entitled to a percentage of his or her final salary depending on factors such as years of service. The vast majority of all new pension schemes are on a defined contribution basis, which effectively transfers the investment risk from the employer to the individual.

The Pensions Board explained the rationale for this change in its 1998 document: 'Almost all new schemes are being set up as defined contribution schemes for the reasons of predictability of cost, fewer regulatory requirements, transparency and influence of United States companies locating in Ireland' (Pensions Board, 1998: 5).

Table A1: The change in pension fund provision

	Defined benefit		Defined contribution	
	No. of schemes	No. of members	No. of schemes	No. of members
December 1995	2,137	406,906	42,565	78,974
December 2000	2,027	449,111[*]	84,321	180,690

Source: Annual Reports of the Pensions Board.
* Approximately half are in the public sector.

The change to a system of defined contribution has benefits as well as additional risk for individuals. The benefits include a far greater level of personal flexibility in both career choice and the type of assets that individuals can purchase. The risk arises from the lack of a guarantee in the level of income because of the uncertainty over the value of the assets upon retirement.[53]

The government has introduced Personal Savings Retirement Accounts (PRSAs) as part of the Pensions Bill, 2001. These have a similar philosophy to defined contribution funds, with individuals having responsibility for investing their own funds.

Ireland is not alone in changing the structure of pension provision. A wide range of OECD countries are making similar arrangements where over time the state is transferring responsibility for pension provision to the individual (Myles and Pierson, 2001).

The significance of these changes for financial regulation has not received the attention it deserves. There will be an increased role for the IFSRA as individuals buy and sell assets or investment funds for their pension, rather than delegate responsibility to their employer. There will be an accompanying increased requirement for education so that individuals have the ability to understand the complexities of the products and the risks involved.[54] The personal pension mis-selling scandal in the UK that affected an estimated two-three million investors and has cost the financial sector more than £11 billion sterling is a particularly alarming example for regulators and governments (quoted in Davies, 2000).

The IFSRA will have a role in ensuring that individuals have access to information about the issues and in regulating the institutions that sell the investment products. The long-term public policy concern for government arises if individuals, for whatever reason, do not have sufficient income to fund their retirement and the subsequent implications for the public finances.

---

[53] The level of risk with a defined contributions scheme is illustrated by a study undertaken by actuaries Lane, Clark and Peacock that shows an individual in Britain retiring in 1972 at the age of sixty-five received 65 per cent of final salary while an individual that retired in 1974 at the same age received only 25 per cent, *Financial Times*, 17 June, 2000.

[54] See Schiller (2000:218) 'Curious lack of public concern about this risk'.

Shift in personal assets

The change in pension fund provision has been compounded by a shift in the nature of the financial assets that Irish people own. There is a lack of comprehensive data on the subject, but there is a clear trend towards the ownership of what may be termed 'risk' assets.

A survey by Goodbody Stockbrokers (2000) has estimated that 17 per cent of individuals own stocks directly,[55] but in the United States nearly 50 per cent of American citizens have exposure to stocks.[56]

The Irish Association of Investment Managers has estimated that IR£1.7 billion of investment funds were purchased in 2000, of which approximately IR£1.2 billion may be termed risk assets.[57] The purchase of an investment fund allows the individual to delegate to a financial institution the decision about what type of 'risk asset' is purchased.

The purchase of such assets reflects a combination of factors, including a desire to make provision for retirement and the perceived attraction of higher returns available from equity products as opposed to 'safe' bank and building society deposits.

The shift in the risk-profile of the assets that individuals are purchasing may well be a case of 'caveat emptor', in so far as individuals are making these decisions on a voluntary basis. However, there is a need to educate people about the nature of the risk that they are undertaking.

---

[55] This figure does not include indirect holdings in pension funds or insurance companies which are managed by financial institutions.

[56] Some 48.2 per cent of US households own stocks either in mutual funds or directly according to a survey by the Securities Industry Organization and the Investment Companies Institute. The survey was published in October 2000 and is available at http://www.ici.org.

[57] This figure does not include cash and fixed-income funds.

Appendix 2

The accountability documents of the New Zealand securities commission

Work Programme effective 1 July 2000
Our Work Programme for the year is set out below, divided into six categories and including, for each category, estimate of percentage of total expenditure for the year.

Category 1: Exemptions
1 Receive and consider applications
2 Review exemptions
   - review selected existing exemptions
   - revoke exemptions no longer needed.
3 Special projects
   - simplify offer procedures for small businesses
   - facilitate offers by overseas collective investment schemes.

Estimated expenditure: 26%

Category 2: Market authorisations
4 Futures and options contracts
   - authorise futures dealers
   - consider amendments to Exchange rules
   - review policies for dealer authorisations.
5 Trustees and statutory supervisors
   - approve trustees and statutory supervisors
   - review terms and conditions of approval.
6 Share dealing
   - designate money market entities for relief from the substantial security holder disclosure rules.

7   Securities transfer
-    receive and consider applications for approval of
     electronic systems.

Estimated expenditure: 2%

Category 3: Enforcement

8   Observe securities market activity
-    prospectuses and investment statements
-    advertisements
-    financial statements
-    disclosure of substantial security holdings
-    insider trading
-    market manipulation
-    company takeovers and compulsory acquisitions
-    corporate governance
-    funds management
-    investment advice.

9   Conduct inquiries and initiate action on:
-    prospectuses, investment statements and
     advertisements for securities, insider trading
     including the application of statutory procedures for
     considering allegations of malpractice
-    substantial security holder disclosure including
     applications to the High Court in respect of non-
     disclosure of prescribed information
-    the financial statements of public issuers
-    the practices of investment advisers
-    requests from overseas securities commissions.

10   Registrar of Companies:
-    requests to/from the Registrar for inspection of the
     documents of issuers and promoters of securities
     and investment advisers
-    requests for the exercise of powers under the
     Corporations (Investigations and Management) Act
-    appeals against the decisions of the Registrar.

Estimated expenditure: 40%

Category 4: Reform

11   Securities Act and Regulations review aspects of Securities Act 1978, in particular,
- administrative and efficiency aspects, possible wider exemption powers, who is 'the public', small and medium-sized enterprises (SMEs)
- work with the Ministry of Commerce in their review of the Securities Regulations 1983.

12   Electronic offers
- to review practices and procedures for the communication of offer documents by electronic means.

13   Financial reporting of Public Issuers
- review and comment on exposure drafts for financial reporting standards of the Institute of Chartered Accountants of New Zealand and the Accounting Standards Review Board
- review and comment on International Organisation of Securities Commissions (IOSCO) proposals for the promotion of international accounting standards.

14   Insider trading
- consider possible exemption power for Securities Commission in respect of liability.

15   Substantial security holders
- review of rules of law about substantial security holder disclosure and make recommendations for reform.

16   Funds management practice
- review aspects of funds management practice and release discussion paper.

17   Power to make rulings
- prepare discussion paper on possible power for the Commission give binding rules on application of securities law.

18   Fair trading and consumer guarantees act
- review application to securities and futures contracts.

Estimated expenditure: 11%

Category 5: International liaison
   19   IOSCO projects
       -    work with the IOSOCO, including projects on
            • objectives and principles of securities regulation
            • competition policy
            • securities regulation.
   20   Cross border offers of securities
       -    promote improved communication on
            • overseas regulatory practices
            • market malpractice, in particular in respect of
              cross border offers of securities.
   Estimated expenditure: 10%

Category 6: Public understanding
   21   Communication
       -    publish regular Commission bulletins
       -    publish exemption notes
       -    present speeches, papers, reports
       -    correspond and engage generally in telephone and
            other electronic communication
       -    manage the website
       -    maintain contacts with the news media
       -    education project.
   Estimated expenditure: 11%

Statement of service
Statement of Service Performance (for the year ended 30 June 2000)

A. Performance Standards and Measures
Category 1: Exemptions
To consider and decide on applications for exemptions from the
provisions of the Securities Act and Regulations.

Outcome. To remove impediments to the offering of securities in
New Zealand and to encourage innovation. To promote confidence
in securities markets.

Quantity. The Commission considered sixty-nine exemption applications (budget ninety applications). It reviewed its procedures for receiving applications.

Quality. The Commission based its work on sensible interpretations of securities laws and their application in a constructive and practical way to securities market practice. It consulted extensively on new policy and on its formal expression in exemption notices. It acted independently and in accordance with the law.

Timeliness. The Commission gave priority to all exemption work. It completed individual items of work within reasonable timetables set by market participants. The only exception to this was in respect of an exemption application for overseas collective investment schemes. This raised wider policy questions affecting the community generally and there was a need for public consultation.

Cost. The Commission allocated 29% (budget 32%) of its expenditure to this output.

Category 2: Market authorisations

To consider and decide on applications for authorisation of market participants, for example futures exchanges and dealers, trustees and statutory supervisors.

Outcome. To secure minimum standards for specified classes of people undertaking securities market business. To encourage innovation and to promote confidence in securities markets.

Quantity. Considered ten applications (budget six applications) for authorisation.

Quality. The Commission considered applications in accordance with legal requirements including, where appropriate, the rules of natural justice. It based its work on sensible interpretations of securities laws and their application in a constructive and practical way to securities market practice. It acted independently.

Timeliness. The Commission gave priority to authorisation work. It completed items of work within reasonable timetables set by market participants.

Cost. The Commission allocated 1% (budget 2%) of its expenditure to this output.

Category 3: Enforcement
To observe securities market activity and to intervene in the interests of investors in accordance with statutory powers.

Outcome. To improve standards of behaviour in securities markets and to improve compliance with securities law.

Quantity. The Commission completed sixty-five enforcement inquiries (budget fifty inquiries) of which one was a major inquiry involving 630 hours of Commission time. It approved the prohibition of three company directors and managers (budget five approvals).

Quality. The Commission acted in response to market needs and in accordance with legal requirements including, where appropriate, the rules of natural justice. It based its work on sensible interpretations of securities laws and their application in a constructive and practical way to securities market practice. It acted independently. It tested its performance against the comments of the media and professional advisers to market participants.

Timeliness. The following enforcement work was treated as urgent and actioned immediately:

- all proposals to suspend prospectus or investment statements or to prohibit advertisements
- all requests for the Registrar of Companies to inspect the documents of issuers or promoters of securities or the investment advisers associated with them.

Subject to resources and work priorities the Commission completed other enforcement work promptly. By doing this it minimised the commitment of resources by both market participants and the Commission. It ensured, where appropriate, that results were communicated promptly to market participants and the public generally.

Cost. The Commission allocated 35% (budget 36%) of its expenditure to this output.

Category 4: Reform
To review securities law and market practice, both domestically and across international frontiers, and to make recommendations for reform.

Outcome. To improve the operation of securities law and established market practice both domestically and across international frontiers. To enhance New Zealand's reputation both domestically and overseas as a co-operative and well-regulated country. To keep abreast of developments in both domestic and global standard setting and to contribute our views on this.

Quantity. The Commission issued statements or comments or reports on eighteen matters (budget twenty). Of these fifteen matters related to the development of the New Zealand market and three matters related to co-operation with IOSCO and overseas securities commissions, and the development of global policies, codes of conduct and standards of behaviour.

Very little work related to law reform, in particular to improvements to New Zealand statute law or regulation. Our resources for this are slender and the Ministry of Commerce is ultimately responsible for advice to the government. The only significant new law reform project was a study, not yet completed, on a possible power for the Commission to give binding rulings on the application of securities law to market situations.

Quality. The Commission complied with its obligations under the Securities Act 1978 and with other relevant legislation. It based its work on sensible interpretations of securities laws and their application in a constructive and practical way to securities market practice. It secured widespread interest overseas in its views on the emerging IOSCO statement on the Objectives and Principles of Securities Regulation. It acted independently.

Timeliness. The Commission met the timetables of all those to whom its communications were addressed.

Cost. The Commission allocated 22% (budget 20%) of its expenditure to this output. Of this some 10% of expenditure related to international matters.

Category 5: Public understanding
To promote public understanding of the law and practice of securities.

Outcome. To increase the community's awareness and understanding of securities market practice, the policy of the law, and the importance of the Commission's work.

Quantity. The Commission published a quarterly bulletin. It produced speeches, papers and reports as appropriate. It continued to develop the website, in particular, by publishing exemption notes. The Commission supported other bodies promoting public understanding. It communicated regularly with the media and the public.

Quality. We surveyed recipients of the bulletin on the quality and content of the publication. We conclude that it is useful and well regarded by those who replied to our survey. Public use of the website increased steadily. We based our work on observed market practice and sensible interpretations of the law.

Timeliness. The Commission met production deadlines for the quarterly bulletin and other public understanding projects.

Cost. The Commission allocated 13% (budget 10%) of its expenditure to this output.

B. General observations

Governance
The Commission members are appointed by the governor-general on the recommendation of the minister having regard to their qualifications, experience, skill and reputation for integrity in the public market for securities. New appointments are made only after extensive advertising in the newspapers.

All aspects of our work were kept under continuing review by regular reporting to Commission members, by the frequent meetings of the Commission, a total of 127 during the 2000 financial year (twelve regular monthly meetings and 115 quorum meetings including telephone conferences with decisions confirmed by resolutions in writing), and by supervision of staff by the chief executive.

Where matters of significant policy arose at quorum meetings they were referred to a full meeting for further consideration by all Commission members.

The Commission reported quarterly to the Minister for Enterprise and Commerce.

Work priorities

We reviewed our priorities at each monthly meeting of the Commission and our complete work programme quarterly.

We assessed all requests for new work promptly. Where we were unable to undertake work, because it was not within the Commission's terms of reference, because it was not within our established priorities or because we believed another agency might be able to provide more relevant or more effective service, we said so promptly.

Priority was given to work on exemptions and authorisations. We needed to ensure that the activities of market participants were not delayed or inhibited because we were not able to provide a prompt, relevant and effective service.

Priority was given under enforcement

- to proposals to suspend prospectuses or investment statements and prohibit advertisements containing offers of securities to the public where these were thought to be misleading
- to the requests of the Registrar of Companies, particularly requests to inspect documents of issuers or promoters of securities.

Priority was given under Reform to the IOSCO Objectives and Principles of Securities Regulation and to the IOSCO Implementation Committee on the Objectives and Principles of Securities Regulation.

Priority was given to all core aspects of our work on public understanding.

We believe that much of our work could be completed more quickly if the procedures prescribed in the Securities Act 1978 for the administration of business, for example the procedures for meetings and the delegation of responsibilities, were simplified. We have made certain recommendations to the government on this.

Source: New Zealand Securities Commission, at http://www.sec-com.govt.nz/about/who

References

Ahern, B. (2002), *Irish Times*, p.18, 28 February 2002.

Alliance for Investor Education, at www.investoreducation.org.

Australian Securities and Investment Commission, at www.asic.government.au.

Aviation Regulation Bill (2000), Dublin: Stationery Office.

Boston, J. (ed.) (1991), *Reshaping the State: New Zealand's Bureaucratic Revolution*, Auckland/Oxford: Oxford University Press.

Boyle, R. (1998), *Governance and Accountability in the Civil Service*, CPMR Discussion Paper 6, Dublin: Institute of Public Administration.

Boyle, R. and S. Fleming (2000), *The Role of Strategy Statement*, CPMR Research Report 2, Dublin: Institute of Public Administration.

Brennan, S. (2000), Minister of State at the Department of the Taoiseach: *A New Dáil for the New Millennium*, November 2000, Dublin: Department of the Taoiseach.

Briault, C. (1999), 'The Rationale for a Single National Financial Services Regulator', Occasional Paper, London: Financial Services Authority.

Briault, C. (2002), 'Revisiting the Rationale for a Single National Financial Services Regulator', Occasional Paper, London: Financial Services Authority.

Byrne, D. (1998), UCD Law Society, November 12, 1998, Dublin: Attorney General's Office.

Byrne, D. (2000), Speech to the Institute of European Affairs, 28 January, 2000, Dublin: Institute of European Affairs.

Cabinet Office (1999), *Modernising Government*, March 1999, London: Stationery Office.

Central Bank and Financial Services Authority of Ireland Bill (2002), Dublin: Stationery Office.

Central Bank of Ireland (2001), *Annual Report*, Dublin: Central Bank of Ireland.

Centre for Economic Policy Research (2000), *One Money, Many Countries: Monitoring the ECB*, February 2000, London: Centre for Economic Policy Research.

Coakley, J. and M. Gallagher (eds) (1999), *Politics in the Republic of Ireland*, third edition, London: Routledge.

Commission for Electricity Regulation (1999), *Submission to Minister for Public Enterprise*, November 1999, Dublin.

Committees of the Houses of the Oireachtas (Compellability, Privileges and Immunities of Witnesses) Act, 1997, Dublin: Stationery Office.

Committee of Public Accounts (1999), *Parliamentary Inquiry into DIRT*, First Report, Vol. 1, December 1999, Dublin: Stationery Office.

Committee of Public Accounts (2000), minutes of meeting, 3 February, 2000, Dublin: Houses of the Oireachtas.

Communications Regulation Act (2002), Dublin: Stationery Office.

Competition Authority (1999), Response of the Competition Authority to the Competition and Mergers Review Group's proposals for discussion in relation to competition law, Dublin: Competition Authority.

Competition Authority, at www.irlgov.ie/compauth.

Comptroller and Auditor General (1999a), *Report on Impact of Value for Money Examinations 1994-1996*, November 1999, Dublin: Stationery Office.

Comptroller and Auditor General (1999b), *Report on Evaluation of Effectiveness: Central Bank Financial Regulation*, December 1999, Dublin: Stationery Office.

Consumer Panel of the FSA (2000), Annual Report (2000), at www.fs-cp.org/public/pdf010315, London: Financial Services Authority.

Davies, H. (2000), Chairman of the Financial Services Authority: Speech at International Organisation Securities Commission (IOSCO), 17 May, 2000, London: FSA.

Day, P. and R. Klein (1987), *Accountabilities*, London: Tavistock.

Department of Enterprise, Trade and Employment (2000), *Strategy Statement 2001-2003*, at www.entemp.ie/, Dublin.

Department of Finance (1998), *Strategy Statement 1998-2000*, Dublin: Department of Finance.

Department of Finance (2000), *Strategy Statement 2001-2003*, Dublin: Department of Finance.

Department of Finance (2001), 'A New Structure for Financial Regulation in Ireland', February 2001, Dublin: Department of Finance.

Department of Public Enterprise (2000a), *Governance and Accountability in the Regulatory Process: Policy Proposals*, March 2000, Dublin: Department of Public Enterprise.

Department of Public Enterprise (2000b), *Outline Legislative Proposals in Relation to the Regulation of the Communications Sector*, September 2000, Dublin: Department of Public Enterprise.

Department of Social, Community and Family Affairs (1998), *Interim Report on Implementation of Customer Action Plan 1998-1999*, Dublin: Department of Social, Community and Family Affairs.

Department of the Taoiseach (1999), 'Reply to Another Set of Strategy Statements: What is the Evidence on Implementation?', *Administration*, Volume 47, No. 1 (Spring 1999), Dublin: Institute of Public Administration.

Department of the Taoiseach (2000), *Strategy for the Development of the International Financial Services Industry in Ireland*, Progress Report, Dublin: Department of the Taoiseach.

Director of Telecommunications Regulation (2000), *Submission to Joint Oireachtas Committee on Public Enterprise and Transport: April 6, 2000*, Dublin: Office of the Director of Telecoms Regulation.

Dooney, S. and J. O'Toole (1999), *Irish Government Today*, Dublin: Gill and Macmillan.

Doyle, E. (2000), Address to Joint Oireachtas Committee on Public Enterprise and Transport, 6 April, 2000. Dublin.

Electricity Regulation Act (1999), Dublin: Stationery Office.

Financial Services Authority, at www.fsa.government.uk, London.

Financial Services Authority (2000), *New Regulator for a New Millennium*, January 2000, London: FSA.

Financial Services Authority (2002a), *FSA Plan and Budget 2002/03*, London: FSA.

Financial Services Authority (2002b), *Our Approach to Performance Evaluation*, London: FSA.

Financial Services Industry Association (2001), *Annual Report*, Dublin: FSIA.

Fingleton, J. (1999), *Arrangements in the Regulatory Process*, Prepared for the Office of the ODTR, National Economic Research Associates, November 1999, Dublin: ODTR.

Fingleton, J., J. Evans and O. Hogan (1998), *The Dublin Taxi Market: Re-regulate or Stay Queuing?*, Dublin: The Policy Institute.

Foot, Michael (2000), 'Our New Approach to Risk-Based Regulation – What Will Be Different for Firms', London: Financial Services Authority.

Financial Services Authority (2000), press release, March 2000, at www.fsa.gov.uk/pubs/press/2000.

Gallagher, M. (1999), 'Parliament', in Coakley, J. and M. Gallagher (eds) (1999), *op.cit.*

Goodbody Stockbrokers (2000), 'Private Share Ownership in Ireland: the future after eircom', April 2000, Dublin.

Hennessy, P. (1996), *Muddling Through: power, politics and the quality of government in postwar Britain*, London: Gollancz.

House of Commons Treasury Committee Report (1999), February 1999, London.

Humphreys, P. (1998), *Improving Public Service Delivery Systems*, CPMR Discussion Paper No. 7, Dublin: Institute of Public Administration.

International Monetary Fund (February 2001), *Report on the Observance of Standards and Codes* at www.imf.org/external/np/rosc/irl/index.

Irish Association of Investment Managers (1998), Submission to the Implementation Advisory Group on the Establishment of a Single Regulatory Authority for the Financial Services Sector, December 1998, Dublin.

Joint Committee of Enterprise and Economic Strategy (1996), *Oireachtas Report*, October 1996, Dublin: Houses of the Oireachtas.

Joint Committee on Enterprise and Economic Strategy (1997a), minutes of meeting, 7 January, 1997, Dublin: Houses of the Oireachtas.

Joint Committee on Enterprise and Economic Strategy (1997b), minutes of meeting, 8 January, 1997, Dublin: Houses of the Oireachtas.

Joint Committee on Enterprise and Economic Strategy (1997c), *Report of the Select Committee on Enterprise and Economic Strategy on the Regulation of Investment Intermediaries*, April 1997, Dublin: Houses of the Oireachtas.

Joint Committee on Finance and the Public Service (1998a), 1 April, 1998, minutes of meeting, p. 65, Dublin: Houses of the Oireachtas

Joint Committee on Finance and the Public Service (1998b), *The Regulation and Supervision of Financial Institutions*, July 1998, Dublin: Houses of the Oireachtas.

Joint Committee on Finance and the Public Service (1999), *Report of meeting on Report of the Implementation Advisory Group on the Establishment of a Single Regulatory Authority for the Financial Services Sector*, October 1999, Dublin: Houses of the Oireachtas.

Joint Committee on Finance and the Public Service (2000), *Draft Report of meeting on report of the Implementation Advisory Group on the Establishment of a Single Regulatory Authority*, February 2000, Dublin: Houses of the Oireachtas.

Joint Committee on Financial Services and Markets (1999), *First Report on Establishment of the Financial Services Authority* (April 1999), London: House of Commons.

Joint Committee on Financial Services and Markets (1999), *Second Report on establishment of the Financial Services Authority* (May/June 1999), London: House of Commons.

Kearney, C. (October 1999), 'Medium-Term Prospects for the Irish Financial System', *Medium Term Review*, Economic and Social Research Institute, No. 7, Dublin: ESRI.

Keller, M. (1990), *Regulating a New Economy*, Cambridge: Harvard University Press.

Keogan J.F. and D. McKevitt (1997), 'Making Sense of Strategy Statements: A User's Guide', *Administration*, Volume 43, No. 2, Dublin: Institute of Public Administration.

Keogan, J.F. and D. McKevitt (1999), 'Another Set of Strategy Statements: What is the Evidence on Implementation?' *Administration*, Volume 47, No.1, 1999, Dublin: Institute of Public Administration.

Kettl, D. (2000), *The Global Public Management Revolution*, Washington DC: Brookings.

Laver, M. (1996), 'Notes on a New Irish Senate', in *Report of the Constitution Review Group* (May 1996), Dublin: Stationery Office.

Levitt, A. (2001), Speech, 16 January, 2001, at www.sec.gov/news/speech/spch457.htm, Washington DC: Securities and Exchange Commission.

Llewellyn, D. (1999), *The Economic Rationale for Financial Regulation*, FSA Occasional Paper, April 1999, London: Financial Services Authority.

Longley, L. and R. Davidson (eds) (1998), *The New Roles of Parliamentary Committees*, Ilford, England: Frank Cass.

Majone, G. (ed.) (1996), *Regulating Europe*, London and New York: Routledge.

March, J. and J.Olsen, (1995), *Democratic Governance*, New York: Free Press.

McDowell, M. (1999), Speech to the Irish Association of Corporate Treasurers, 30 October, 1999, Dublin: Attorney General's Office.

McDowell, M. (2000), Address to University College Cork Law Society, 10 February, 2000, Dublin: Attorney General's Office.

McKevitt, D. and A. Lawton (1994), *Public Sector Management, Theory, Critique and Practice*, London: The Open University.

Mullarkey, P. (1998), Evidence to Joint Committee on Finance and the Public Service (April 1998), in *Report of the Implementation Advisory Group on the Establishment of a Single Regulatory Authority for the Financial Services Sector* (1999), *op.cit.*

Myles, J. and P. Pierson (2001), in Pierson, Paul (ed.), *op.cit.*

National Audit Office (2000), *Good Practice in Performance Reporting in Executive Agencies and Non-Departmental Public Bodies*, March 2000, Report by the Comptroller and Auditor General, London: Stationery Office.

National Council for Curriculum and Assessment (1999), *Civic, Social and Political Education*, Guidelines for Teachers, The Junior Certificate, Dublin: NCEA.

New Zealand State Services Commission (1999), Crown Entities: Reviews of Statement of Intent, Occasional Paper 20 (September 1999), New Zealand: State Services Commission.

New Zealand State Services website, at www.ssc.government.nz.

Norton, P. (1998) (ed.), *Parliaments and Government in Western Europe*, Ilford, England: Frank Cass.

O'Halpin, E. (1998), *A Changing Relationship? Parliament and Government in Ireland*, chapter in Norton (ed.), *op.cit.*

Office of the Clerk of the House of Representatives (New Zealand) (2000), *Effective Select Committee Membership: A Guide for Members of Parliament*, Wellington.

Office of the Director of Telecommunications Regulation (1999), *Market Regulators: Governance and Accountability – Response to the Minister for Public Enterprise*, (November 1999), Dublin: ODTR.

Office of the Director of Telecommunications Regulation (2000), 'Response to the outline legislative proposals', Dublin: ODTR.

Office of the House of the Oireachtas, *Statement of Strategic Objectives 1996-1999* (December 1996), Dublin: Stationery Office.

Oftel Consumer Panel, at www.oftel.gov.uk.

Oireachtas Report (1989), debate on the Central Bank Act of 1989, p. 1913-1918, Oireachtas Report, Dublin: Houses of the Oireachtas.

OECD (1996), *Performance Auditing and the Modernisation of Government*, Paris: OECD.

OECD (1997a), *Report on Regulatory Reform: Summary*, Paris: OECD.

OECD (1997b), *In Search of Results: Performance Management Practices*, Paris: OECD.

OECD (1997c), *The OECD Report on Regulatory Reform: Synthesis*, Paris: OECD.

OECD (1997d), *The OECD Report on Regulatory Reform*, Vol. 1: Sectoral Studies, Paris: OECD.

OECD (2001), *Regulatory Reform in Ireland*, Paris: OECD.

O'Rourke, M. (2000), *The Irish Times*, 19 May 2000, p. 6.

Osborne D., and R Gaebler (1993), *Reinventing Government*, New York: Plume.

Pensions Board (1998), 'Securing Retirement Income', National Pensions Policy Initiative, Report of the Pensions Board, May 1998, Dublin: Pensions Board.

Peters, B. Guy (1996), *Governing – Four Emerging Models*, Kansas: University Press of Kansas.

Peterson, P. (1999), *The Gray Dawn*, New York: Random House.

Pierson, P. (ed.) (2001), *The New Politics of the Welfare State*, Oxford: Oxford University Press.

Public Services Management Act (1997), Dublin: Stationery Office.

Report of the Constitution Review Group (1996), May 1996, Dublin: Stationery Office.

Report of the Implementation Advisory Group on the Establishment of a Single Regulatory Authority for the Financial Services Sector (1999), May 1999, Dublin: Government Publications.

Report of the Joint Committee on Public Enterprise and Transport (1998), Meeting with the Director of Telecommunications Regulation (October 1998), Dublin: Houses of the Oireachtas.

Report of the Oireachtas Joint Committee on Finance and the Public Service (1998), (1 April, 1998), Dublin: Houses of the Oireachtas.

Report of the Select Committee on Enterprise and Economic Strategy on the Regulation of Investment Intermediaries, (1997), Dublin: Stationery Office.

Response of the Competition Authority to invitation to comment on governance and accountability arrangements in the regulatory process (1999), November 1999, Dublin: Competition Authority.

Revenue Commissioners (2001), *Statistical Bulletin 2000*, Dublin: Revenue Commissioners.

Rhodes, R. (1997), *Understanding Governance*, London: Open University Press.

Schiller, R. (2000), *Irrational Exuberance*, Princeton: Princeton

University Press.
Second Report to Government of the Co-ordinating Group of Secretaries (1996), *Delivering Better Government*, Dublin: Stationery Office.
Stagg, E. TD, Speaking on the Electricity Regulation Bill, 3 February, 1999, Dublin: Oireachtas Report.
Stigler, G. (1971), 'The Theory of Economic Regulation', *Bell Journal of Economics and Management*, Vol. 2, no.1, pp. 3-21.
Telecommunications Miscellaneous Provisions Act (1996), Dublin: Stationery Office.
Thatcher, M. and A. Stone Stewart (2002), 'Theories and Practice of Delegation to Non-Majoritarian Institutions', *Western European Politics*, Vol. 25, No. 1, January 2002, London: Frank Cass.
The Treasury (1998), *Public Services for the Future: Modernisation, Reform, Accountability*, London: Stationery Office.
The Treasury (1999), Public Service Agreements: March 1999, Supplement, London: Stationery Office.
Verheijen, T. and M. Millar (1998), 'Reforming public policy processes and securing accountability: Ireland in a comparative perspective', *International Review of Administrative Sciences*, Vol. 64, 1998, London: Sage Publications.
Vogel, S. K. (1996), *Freer Markets, More Rules: Regulatory Reform in Advanced Industrial Countries*, Ithaca and London: Cornell University Press.
Working Group on Banking and Consumer Issues (1998), *Report* (October 1998), Department of Finance (released under Freedom of Information Act), Dublin.